your visit to
ORSAY

ARCHITECTURE
SCULPTURE
PAINTING
GRAPHIC ARTS
PHOTOGRAPHY
CINEMATOGRAPHY
DECORATIVE ARTS

ORIGINAL TEXT WRITTEN BY VALÉRIE METTAIS

art lys ♪

Cover: Vincent Van Gogh, *Self-Portrait*, Saint-Rémy-de-Provence, 1889. Oil on canvas, 65 x 54.5 cm.
Pages 8 and 9: central aisle of the Musée d'Orsay

EDITORIAL CO-ORDINATION: DENIS KILIAN
GRAPHIC DESIGN AND LAYOUT: MARTINE MÈNE
PLANS: THIERRY LEBRETON, DOMINIQUE BISSIÈRE
PICTURE RESEARCH: CHRISTIAN RYO
PRODUCTION: PIERRE KEGELS

CONTENTS

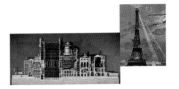

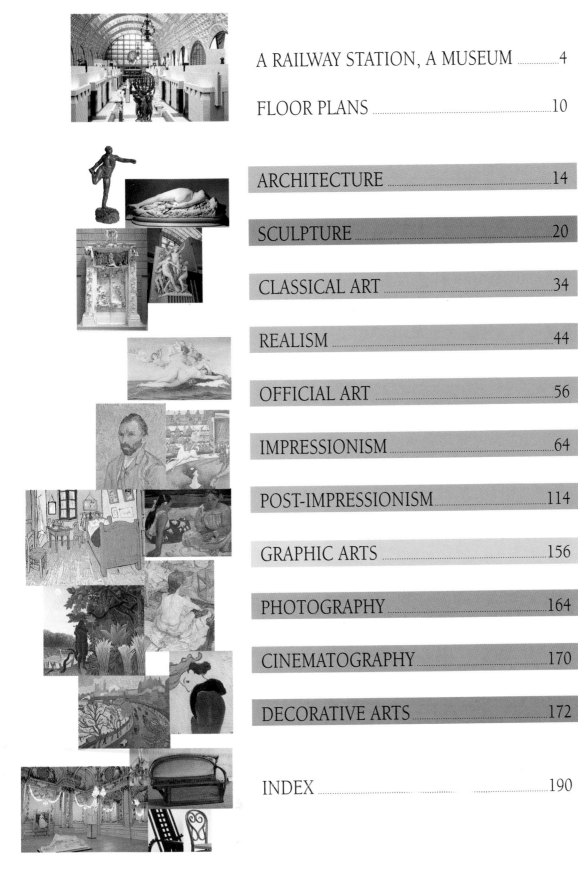

A RAILWAY STATION, A MUSEUM

At the end of last century, the *Compagnie des Chemins de Fer d'Orléans* purchased a piece of land on which stood the ruins of two buildings that had been burnt down during the Commune insurrection in 1871, namely the cavalry barracks and the Palais d'Orsay, former seat of the Court of Auditors and the Council of State. It was a prime location, in an elegant quarter at the heart of Paris, by the Seine, facing the Tuileries and, a little further away, the Louvre. It was an obvious choice for the terminus serving the south-west of France, which had until then been situated at the Gare d'Austerlitz. The story of the Gare d'Orsay thus began.

IMMENSE AND MODERN

A competition was organised and, of the three architects consulted, the contract was awarded to Victor Laloux. Winner of the *Grand Prix de Rome*, a master of turn-of-the-century eclecticism, capable of bringing together different styles, periods and sources of inspiration, and concealing the metal structures behind a stone façade, his plans were accepted on April 21, 1898. There was very little time since the Universal Exhibition had been planned for 1900. The architect hastened the pace of the work and, over a period of two years, three hundred labourers by day and eighty by night dug fifteen tracks over three thousand six hundred and fifty metres in total.

A colossal, modern passenger railway station was inaugurated on July 14. Colossal in scale: two hundred and twenty metres in length and seventy-five metres wide; a great hall in the form of a nave reaching its highest point at thirty-two metres, with a span of forty metres; twelve thousand tons of metal structures; one hundred and ten thousand square metres of frames, and thirty-five thousand square metres of glass panels… A modern interior, with lifts, goods lifts, and electric engines… Rail traffic would become increasingly heavy during the 20th century, with one hundred and fifty to two hundred daily trains; trains no longer powered by steam, but electricity. What then was the point of building such a large hall which had lost its original function of absorbing smoke from the engines? "As smoke disappears," replied Victor Laloux, "the great railway halls should naturally take on the appearance of large, more luxuriously and comfortably decorated halls." The Gare d'Orsay was above all designed to impress.

ENTIRELY OF STONE, HIGHLY DECORATIVE

A wealth of ornamental décor is displayed both inside and out. At the heart of an elegant quarter, the railway station had to blend into its urban surroundings, show off a façade with pilasters and two neoclassical pavilions, and display rich materials, such as freestone. This railway station would be "colossal, entirely of stone, highly decorative, with boldly pronounced features," emphasised the archi-

View of the Universal Exhibition held in Paris, in 1900.

The Gare d'Orsay at the beginning of the century.

The station interior.

tect, only to reiterate: "Only stone should be visible in the railway station to be built, since only stone is able to replace the Court of Auditors and stand opposite the Tuileries." However, it also needed to stand out to passengers: the seven entrances to the platform, the allegorical statues symbolising the main towns on the railway network, Bordeaux, Toulouse and Nantes, and lastly the large clocks are a few indicators as to the railway activity. "The station is magnificent, and looks like a fine-art pavilion, and since the fine-art pavilion resembles a railway station, I suggest Laloux switches their functions while there is still time," remarked the painter Édouard Detaille in May 1900. The carved, painted staff-coffered ceiling of the nave was inspired by the décor of the Roman thermal baths and basilicas. The hotel adjoining the station was luxuriously decorated and made use of *trompe-l'oeil* effects.

The large clock over the central aisle.

DÉCOR AND GILDING

"The Hôtel du Palais d'Orsay, Quai d'Orsay, is a vast building with an imposing hall where there lingers a sleepy, morning atmosphere. At the reception, we are shown to a room on the second floor. It is laid out very nicely with its small anteroom and adjoining bath, but as far as comfort is concerned it is sadly lacking. One needs a chest of drawers, dash it! We would have gladly swapped the compulsory fireplace with its gilt clock for somewhere to put our underclothes," recollects Thomas Mann in his *Bilan Parisien* of 1926. Rising to five floors and surrounding the gables of the station, the hotel had three hundred and seventy comfortable rooms. Victor Laloux designed and put the finishing touches to the décor of each room, in every single part of the hotel, from the drawing-rooms to the smoking-room; he selected each painter, sculptor and ornamenter, and supervised the entire work.

Tucked away in the *Pavillon Aval*, the reception room overflows with gilding and stuccowork, carved panelling, overdoors and mirrors, strings of lights and other crystal chandeliers. It has been preserved and restored and now houses a few examples of the official art of the Third Republic. The dining-room, painted in bluish tones depicting the charms of the days and seasons, is now the restaurant of the Musée d'Orsay.

View of the Musée d'Orsay from the right bank.

THE DESTRUCTION OF AN OLD BUILDING

The dismal 1930s put an end to the bustling activity of the station. In 1939, one of the pride and joys of the Universal Exhibition had become outdated and unsuitable for the new trains, and the mainline railway service was dissolved. After the war, it was nothing more than a suburban station. The end was in sight: the station was closed down for good. Thus began a long dismal period during which the station, empty and immense, was used for a wide variety of purposes, and after the 1960s awaited certain demolition. It was the setting for *The Trial* filmed by Orson Wells in 1962, and until 1980 the nave was the home of the Renaud-Barrault Theatre Company followed by the auctioneers of the Drouot-Rive Gauche auction house. The station looked as if it would be torn down and replaced by a conference centre and large international hotel. Several projects

The dining-room of the Hôtel de la Gare d'Orsay, now the museum restaurant.

were submitted in 1970, including Le Corbusier's, which was rejected, consisting of a building a hundred or so metres high. However, times changed and 19th-century architecture found favour once again: the façades and décor of the station and hotel were protected by a preservation order in 1973, and then listed in 1978, as the idea of a museum dedicated to the previous century gradually took shape. The Musée d'Orsay's adventures had just begun.

FROM THE REPUBLIC TO THE WAR: 1848-1914

The station needed to be restructured in order to house works of art dating from the second half of the 19th century, representing most spheres and techniques, reflecting all of the different movements whether contemporary, unconscious or opposing, avant-garde or academic, bearing witness to the period between the advent of the Second Republic and declaration of the First World War. 1848-1914: over sixty years of cultural and artistic creations, in their historical context, were to be displayed in a railway station soon to be transformed into a museum, this in itself representing the museum's first masterpiece.

Architecture, sculpture, painting, graphic arts, photography, cinematography and the decorative arts… are all represented; not forgetting music and literature… included in certain exhibitions, and historical themes.

SEARCHING FOR WORK

In order to construct its panoramic perspective, the Musée d'Orsay welcomed national collections from diverse sources: impressionist paintings from the Musée du Jeu de Paume, works of art from the former Musée d'Art Moderne, and many others from the Louvre. It delved into the reserves of museums, town halls and prefectures, in the provinces and in Paris, in search of traces of official art, formerly commissioned by the State, exhibited at the *Salon* and purchased by the Museum of Luxembourg, a "museum for contemporary artists" in the 19th century. Although official art had long been hidden away since decreasing in popularity, it was henceforth invited to hang from the brand new picture rails of the Gare d'Orsay.

The purpose of the various acquisitions was ultimately to fill the empty spaces, particularly with regard to the decorative arts, in the expression of international art nouveau. Purchases, loans, gifts and legacies from patrons or artist inheritances further enriched the museum. The preservation, enhancement and radical transformation of a railway station at the same time added to this multidisciplinary approach.

NEW SPACES, NEW DIRECTIONS

In 1979, the ACT architect agency was selected out of the six architects consulted. Led by Renaud Bardon, Pierre Colboc and Jean-Paul Philippon, a detailed preliminary plan was submitted in 1982, and work started a year later. Their ideas for the restructuring of the space were then joined by those of Gae Aulenti, architect and designer from Milan, responsible for interior design and the museum itinerary, along with fittings and furnishings. The key point was gen-

The central aisle.

View from the Seine sculpture terrace,
on the middle level.

View from the Seine sculpture terrace,
on the middle level.

erally to realign the existing space. While travellers in the 1900s would enter via one of the doorways leading to the platforms, reach the domed vestibule and leave via Rue de Bellechasse, it would be quite different for visitors in the 20th century. Although the northern façade, bordering the Seine, was closed - only one entrance for temporary exhibitions remains -, greater importance was given to the lengthways scope of the building which was reinforced, spreading over the one hundred and thirty-eight metres of the nave – demarcated to the east and west by two tympanums -, in the direction of the former railway tracks. In order to leave the basement free, these were moved under the platform, under the old porch of the railway station. In front of an extended square on Rue de Bellechasse, the large metal awning became the entrance to the museum. Inside, the old premises of the railway station interact with the new rooms of the museum.

The entrance to the museum, Rue de Bellechasse.

AN AISLE, TERRACES, A ROOF...

From the top of the great staircase, visitors are greeted by a projecting view of the museum, discovering beneath the semi-glass vault the central aisle which gradually rises over different levels. Right at the far end, the eye fixes on the vertical forms of two symmetrical towers, closing off the perspective and forming an architectural frame for the monumental sculptures on display, thus so for *The Dance* by Carpeaux. To the east, the *pavillon amont*, one of the two clock pavilions, dedicates its five floors to architecture and the decorative arts. On either side of the royal aisle are rooms over which are terraces. To the north, rooms and terraces open onto the spaces created in the former porch and vestibule, with a view over the Seine. To the south, they lead to other converted rooms in the hotel wing, along Rue de Lille.

Allegories of the Continents, exhibited on the square, on the corner of Rue de Lille and Rue de Bellechasse. Bronzes made for the Universal Exhibition of 1878.

The roof of the vestibule was originally designed for the sole purpose of concealing the nave; not having a floor and constituting a redundant space, it nevertheless revealed a precious quality: an abundance of natural light due to the zenithal glass roof. This light seems to conjure up another, the light of the impressionist paintings which have thus found their place in a suite of rooms at the very top of the museum.

... AND COLOURS

Although the old and the new have begun to interact, the use of colour aims to avoid even the slightest fusion: while the different greens indicate the parts belonging to 19th-century architecture, the dark browns emphasise elements resulting from the following century. The floors and most of the vertical surfaces are covered with Buxy limestone, a light-coloured stone from the Burgundy region, its ochre hues matching the coffers in the vault, restored according to the original design.

View from the Lille sculpture terrace, on the middle level.

After years of research and work, the museum, railway station and hotel unveiled the setting which determined the layout of the collection, spread over three floors, according to a chronological sequence. It was December 1, 1986.

GROUND FLOOR

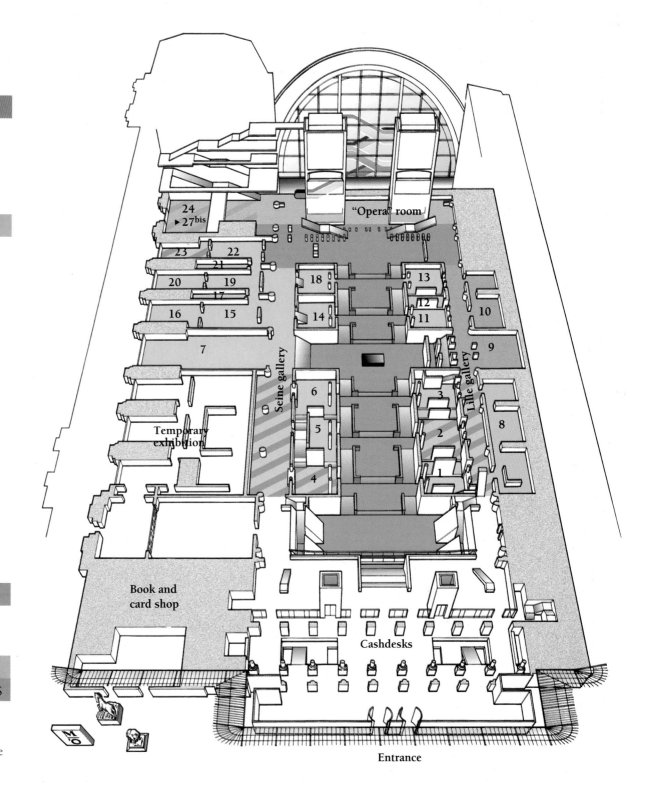

The works are arranged in numbered rooms;
they are occasionally moved or taken away
according to exhibition loans.

UPPER LEVEL

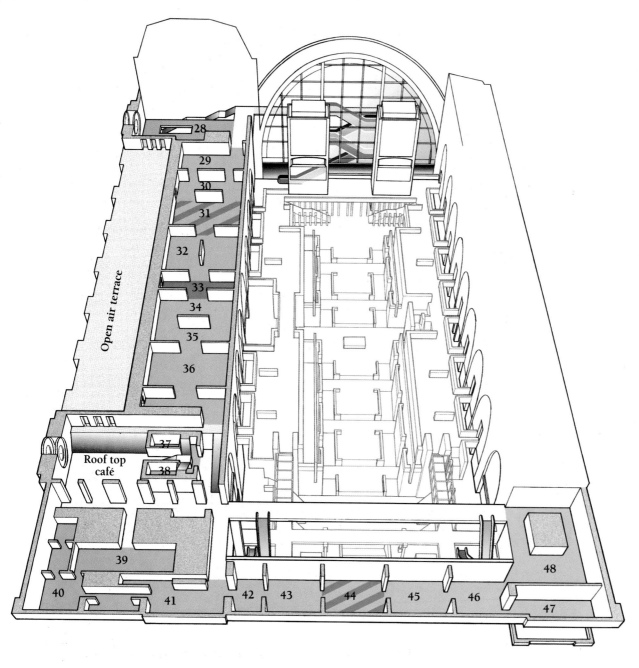

28

29

30

31

32

33

34

35

36

Open air terrace

37

Roof top café

38

39

40   41   42   43   44   45   46   47

48

MIDDLE LEVEL

51 Reception room

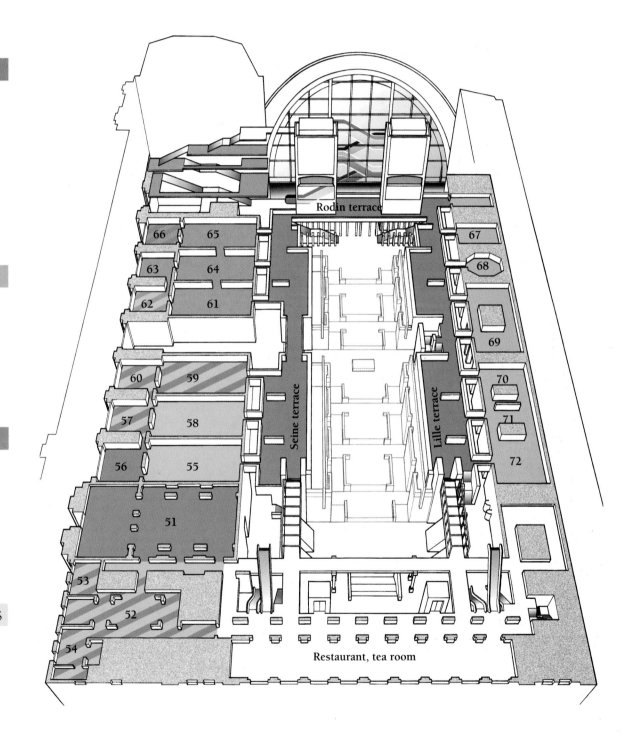

ARCHITECTURE

BRILLIANCE

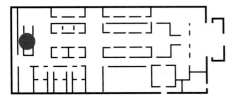

This model is situated on the ground floor, in the Opera room.

When the Paris Opera was inaugurated in 1875, it was the largest in the world, offering singers and dancers a stage twenty-seven metres deep and forty-eight metres wide. There were over two thousand seats for the audience. The architect had resolved not to strive towards unity, both interior and exterior, but rather to assemble and juxtapose different spaces, each thus with its own roof. The route thus starts at the vestibule and, on the first floor, the foyer, then follows the great staircase, enters the auditorium, opposite the stage and its machinery, and finishes in the dance foyer. The dominant theme running throughout is brilliance, marble, granite, porphyry, mosaic, bronze and gold…

THE PARIS OPERA,
by Charles Garnier,
1861-1875.
Model of the longitudinal cross-section of the building, constructed by Atelier in Rome, under the direction of Richard Peduzzi, 1982-1986.

Left: the grand foyer.

Right page: the auditorium.

POLYCHROME DÉCOR

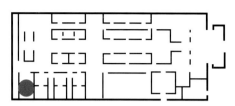

These works are situated
on the ground floor, in room 24.

EUGÈNE VIOLLET-LE-DUC,
*Painted murals
from the chapels of Notre-Dame de Paris,*
circa 1866-1867.
Reliefs reproduced from
the architect's plates.

"To restore a building is not to maintain, repair or redecorate it, it means to bring it back to a state of completion which may have never existed at a given time." This is the definition given in the *Dictionnaire raisonné de l'architecture française*. Its author was the architect Viollet-le-Duc, in charge of major restoration projects during the Second Empire, historian and professor, with a passion for medieval art… His work on Notre-Dame is of interest since it recaptures the place of polychromy in medieval aesthetics, and reveals the importance of coloured surfaces in a cathedral space, emphasising the rhythm of a pillar here and a capital there.

300 METRES, 8000 TONS

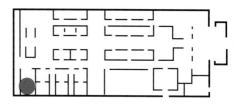

These works belong
to the architecture collections
exhibited on the ground floor
in room 24.

It was erected on Champ-de-Mars in less than two years, from January 28, 1887, the first day of work for the navvies who dug the foundations fifteen metres deep, to March 31, 1889, the inauguration of the Universal Exhibition to commemorate the centenary of the Revolution. From the top of its 320.75 metres and 1710 steps, it dominates Paris, the 8564 tons of its heavy silhouette outlined on the horizon. Two hundred labourers, known as the "carpenters of the sky", assembled and riveted together the metal parts. Engineer Gustave Eiffel's tower was the focal point of great festivities, fireworks and illuminations. It waits serenely for the year 2000 in order to celebrate its one hundred and eleventh anniversary.

View of the Eiffel Tower with, at its feet, a few houses belonging to "The history of human habitats" by Charles Garnier. Cover of Figaro Exposition, 1889.

Opposite:
Tribute to Monsieur Gustave Eiffel. Poster from the Universal Exhibition of 1889.

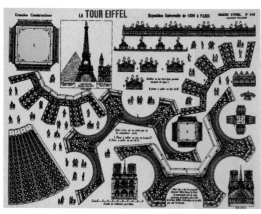

Top:
General view of the Universal Exhibition of 1900.

Above:
CONSTRUCTION SET,
produced for the Universal Exhibition of 1889.

Right page:
Illumination of the Eiffel Tower during the Universal Exhibition of 1889.

SCULPTURE

THE LIFE OF A STATUE

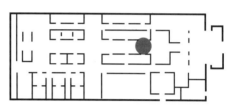

This work is situated on the ground floor, in the central aisle.

Whether draped or bare, belonging to a mere mortal bitten by a serpent or a goddess, the female body was so adored by sculptors that a mythical tale made it the focal point of their art. Pygmalion was king of Cyprus, so the story goes. He carved such a beautiful ivory statue that he fell in love with it and pleaded with the goddess of love and beauty for a wife like it. Venus answered his prayers and that which had been created by a man's hand received a soul. The statue became the wife of the king and was called Galatea.

AUGUSTE CLÉSINGER,
Woman Bitten by a Serpent, 1847.
Marble, l: 180 cm.
The model is Apollonie Aglaé Sabatier,
who inspired many artists of the time.

ECSTASY OF THE DANCE

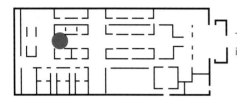

These works are situated on the ground floor, in the central aisle.

JEAN-BAPTISTE CARPEAUX,
The Prince Imperial and His Dog Nero, 1865.
Marble, h: 140 cm.

Right page:
JEAN-BAPTISTE CARPEAUX,
The Dance,
commissioned by Charles Garnier
to decorate the façade of the Opera
1865-1869. Stone, h: 420 cm.
A replica now stands at the Paris Opera.

The Second Empire paid every kind of tribute to Carpeaux. He became the young Prince Eugène Louis' drawing and sculpture master, was esteemed by the Director of Fine Art, the Comte de Nieuwerkerke, and moved in the fashionable circles of Princess Mathilde, cousin of Napoleon III. He was overwhelmed with official commissions: after working on the *Pavillon de Flore* at the Louvre, the sculptor was chosen to collaborate on one of the most emblematic projects of the regime, the Opera. However, not even his imperial patronage could avert scandal and rejection. The allegory of *The Dance* caused a great stir due to the vivid, ecstatic frenzy of his modern maenads.

JEAN-BAPTISTE CARPEAUX,
Ugolino, 1862.
Bronze, h: 194 cm.

IN CLAY AND PLASTER

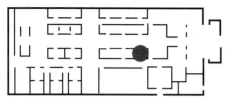

These works are situated on the ground floor, in room 4.

Bloated faces, stiff, hunched-up, grimacing figures with red cheeks. In 1831, Daumier, then aged twenty-three, crudely fashioned a few Louis-Philippesque clay busts, which would serve as sketches for the caricatures that would later appear in *La Caricature* a satirical newspaper. "None such as he has known and loved (in the way of artists) the bourgeois, the last remnant of the Middle Ages, this gothic ruin which refuses to die, this character so ordinary yet so eccentric," wrote Charles Baudelaire admiringly in 1857. In comparison, the treatment of the emigrants, anonymous figures setting out en masse, appears all the more tragic.

HONORÉ DAUMIER, *The Celebrities of the Juste Milieu* or *The Parliamentarians,* 1831.
Thirty-six painted unfired clay busts, h: between 12 and 22 cm.

From left to right: Félix Barthe, Magistrate; Joseph de Podenas, Politician;
Pierre-Paul Royer Collard, Deputy; General Horace-François Sébastiani;
François Guizot, Minister of the Interior; and Auguste de Kératry, Deputy.

HONORÉ DAUMIER, *The Emigrants,* 1848.
Plaster, 28 × 66 cm.

THE MALE BODY

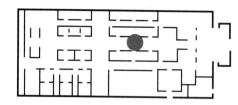

These works are situated on the ground floor, in the central aisle, and on the middle level on the Lille terrace.

For all sculptors, study of the nude is inevitable. Because knowledge of anatomy, both theoretical and practical, is considered the basis of training at the *École des Beaux-Arts*, students work opposite life models and contemplate the lessons left behind by the sculptural forms of antiquity and the Renaissance. Mythical heroes, biblical kings, mere reapers and peasants are some of the subjects enabling the canons of proportion to be thus applied.

EUGÈNE GUILLAUME,
The Reaper, 1849.
Bronze, h: 168 cm.

HIPPOLYTE MOULIN (left),
Find at Pompeii, 1863.
Bronze, h: 187 cm.
ALEXANDRE FALGUIÈRE (right),
Winner of the Cockfight, 1864.
Bronze, h: 174 cm.

Above:
JULES DESBOIS,
Male Torso,
fragment from
The Rock of Sisyphus,
1910. Gilded bronze,
h: 128 cm.

Right page:
ANTONIN MERCIÉ,
David (detail), 1872.
Bronze, h: 184 cm.

WAXEN MODELS

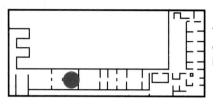

These works are situated
on the upper level,
in room 31.

EDGAR DEGAS,
Dancer Aged Fourteen
from the small class at the Opera
moulded to 3/4 of actual size,
known as *Large Dressed Dancer,*
shown in 1881
at the Sixth Impressionist
Exhibition.
Bronze after
the original wax,
tulle and pink satin, h: 98 cm.

"I make wax models of animals and people for my own pleasure, not simply as a change from painting and drawing, but rather to give my paintings and drawings more expression, ardour and life," Degas told a journalist in 1897. "They are preparatory exercises; nothing more than working documents." Then, "What I need is to express nature in all its character, and movement in its exact truth, to accentuate bone and muscle, and the compact firmness of flesh." After the death of the painter, who made sculptures to improve his painting, his studio revealed some one hundred and fifty models of wax and clay, which had never been exhibited. Only a large dancer had been shown, and had made a vivid impression with its disturbing presence.

EDGAR DEGAS,
Dancer Holding Her Right Foot
With Her Right Hand.
Bronze, h: 53.6 cm.

EDGAR DEGAS,
Dancer Putting on Her Stocking.
Bronze, h: 47 cm.

Top left:
EDGAR DEGAS,
Dancer, Arabesque.
Bronze, h: 40 cm.

FRAGMENTS OF HELL

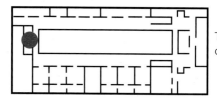

These works are situated on the middle level,
on the Rodin terrace and on the Seine terrace.

AUGUSTE RODIN,
The Gates of Hell,
1880-1917. Plaster,
h: 635 cm.

Left:
AUGUSTE RODIN,
Balzac, 1898.
Plaster, h: 275 cm.
Photograph
by EDWARD STEICHEN,
1908.

"One guesses all of a sudden that to perceive the body as a whole is rather the concern of scientists, whereas the artist uses these elements to create new relationships, new unities, which are greater, more legitimate and more eternal; and this endless richness, this perpetual, infinite inventiveness, this spirit, this purity and vehemence of expression, this youthfulness, this gift of constantly having something else, something better to say, can find no equivalent in human history." In September 1902, Rainer Maria Rilke discovered the sculptor's studio, filled with plaster casts, fragments, studies of contorted, arched, emaciated bodies, an aesthetic to which also belongs the work of Camille Claudel.

CAMILLE CLAUDEL,
Maturity, 1893-1903.
Bronze, h: 114 cm.

THE FULLNESS OF BRONZE

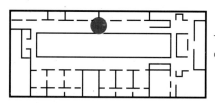

These works are situated on the middle level,
on the Lille terrace.

ÉMILE ANTOINE BOURDELLE,
Hercules the Archer, 1909.
Gilded bronze, h: 248 cm.

Bottom left:
ARISTIDE MAILLOL,
Mediterranean, 1905.
Bronze, h: 110 cm.

Below:
ARISTIDE MAILLOL,
Eve Holding the Apple, 1899.
Bronze, h: 58 cm.

Dark green, brown, black or gilded: bronze lends itself to an infinite number of hues, effects animating the surface, effects of falling light. It is all a matter of proportion, between copper for strength, and tin for better fluidity. With 95% copper, the alloy verges on the red, below 85% it is light yellow; lead is sometimes added. The patina is the ultimate brushstroke, whether natural – simple oxidation colours the metal -, or artificial, fine or dense, concocted with acid solutions. Sculptors, casters and patineurs all have their own carefully guarded secrets.

CLASSICAL ART

STYLE

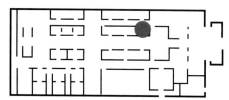

These works are situated on the ground floor, in room 1.

JEAN AUGUSTE DOMINIQUE INGRES,
The Spring, 1820-1856.
Oil on canvas, 163 × 80 cm.

JEAN-LÉON GÉRÔME,
Young Greeks and Fighting Cocks,
1846. Oil on canvas, 143 × 204 cm.

Visiting the Universal Exhibition of 1855 in Paris, Charles Baudelaire stops to ponder over the works of Ingres, the great master of the century, who passed on to his pupils the taste for an ideal of beauty derived from antiquity. He lingers over his quality of line and perception of nature: "carried away by his almost morbid preoccupation with style, the painter often does away with relief or weakens it to such an extent that it becomes invisible, thus hoping to place more emphasis on the contours, so much so that his figures look like rigid models, stuffed with soft, lifeless matter strange to the human body. Occasionally the eye falls upon delightful pieces, irreproachably alive; but a malicious thought then crosses one's mind, that it is not Monsieur Ingres who has sought nature, but nature who has violated the painter, and that this high and mighty woman has subdued him by her compelling influence."

ROMANTICISM AND ORIENTALISM

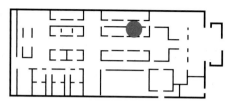

These works are situated on the ground floor, in room 2.

While Eugène Delacroix claimed to have discovered the greatness of antiquity reincarnated in the East during his journey to Morocco in 1832, and while he devoted himself to the passion of savage or cruel scenes, Théodore Chassériau dreamed of Pompeii, where the thermal baths had just been excavated. In a somewhat oriental vision, he imagined the glistening white bodies of those noble Romans as they dried themselves and rested around a brazier after bathing.

EUGÈNE DELACROIX,
The Lion Hunt, sketch from 1854.
Oil on canvas, 86 x 115 cm.

THÉODORE CHASSÉRIAU,
The Tepidarium, 1853.
Oil on canvas, 171 x 258 cm.

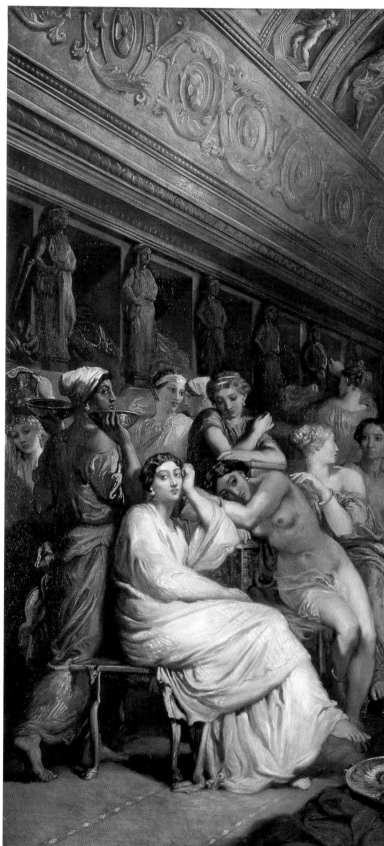

ECLECTICISM

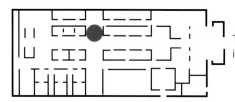

This work is situated on the ground floor, in the central aisle.

THOMAS COUTURE,
Romans of the Decadence, 1847.
Oil on canvas, 472 x 772 cm.

By resolutely turning towards the past and declaring his inordinate ambition "to regenerate art" by studying the masters, Thomas Couture illustrates the concept of "Eclecticism", the art of borrowing, which was to mark the latter half of the 19th century. The result can be seen in these magnificent, decadent Romans. Here, the nudes are meant to be in the style of classical antiquity, following the ideal of beauty of the Greek sculptors; the architecture borrows from Veronese and his *Marriage Feast at Cana*; the range of colours is inspired by Titian, and the brushstroke endeavours to evoke Van Dyck. The subject itself is based on the words of Juvenal, the Roman poet writing in the 1st century AD: "More cruel than war, vice has descended on Rome and avenged the vanquished universe," taken from one of his *Satires*.

BY THE SEA

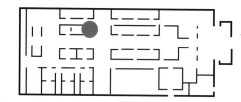

These works are situated on the ground floor, in rooms 11 and 12.

GUSTAVE MOREAU,
Galatea, 1880.
Oil on wood,
85 x 67 cm.

PIERRE PUVIS DE CHAVANNES,
The Poor Fisherman, 1881.
Oil on canvas, 155 x 192 cm.

Right page:
PIERRE PUVIS DE CHAVANNES,
Young Girls by the Sea, 1879.
Oil on canvas, 205 x 154 cm.

Two artists chose to explore the altogether traditional theme of a woman by or in the sea. They approach the theme in utterly different ways. The first depicts partly naked, partly draped figures outlined in blue, pale forms standing out on a marine background with an unreal horizon. The second finds his Galatea in mythology: languishing and fatal, seated in a marine grotto in an array of seaweed, coral and anemones, the sea nymph smoulders under the eye of Polyphemus, a Cyclops enflamed with love. Puvis de Chavannes and Moreau clearly have nothing in common, other than soon being perceived by their contemporaries as different facets of what would become known as Symbolism.

THE LOWLY AND THE REPUBLIC

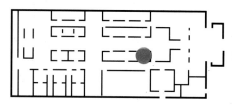

These works are situated on the ground floor, in room 4.

Right page:
HONORÉ DAUMIER, *The Laundress,*
circa 1863. Oil on wood, 49 x 33.5 cm.

HONORÉ DAUMIER, *The Republic,*
Sketch submitted for the exhibition
instituted in 1848 by the *École des Beaux-Arts*
under the Second Republic. Oil on canvas, 73 x 60 cm.

HONORÉ DAUMIER, *The Thieves and the Donkey,*
1858, Oil on canvas, 58.5 x 56 cm.

From caricatures of bourgeois Parisians to scenes of ordinary life, Daumier was a great observer of his time. The artist lived through several regimes, from the reign of Louis-Philippe – during which he served six months in prison for publishing a drawing that ridiculed the king – to the early days of the Third Republic. From errand boy to bookshop assistant, he tried every trade before devoting himself to lithography, drawing, painting and sculpture. Daumier was very versatile. Acclaimed by Baudelaire and Delacroix, upheld by Millet and Corot, and esteemed by Van Gogh, Daumier's work earned the admiration of several generations. Nonetheless, he still died in poverty in 1879.

REALISM

IMAGES OF THE LAND

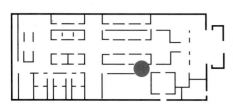

These works are situated on the ground floor, in the Seine gallery.

CHARLES-FRANÇOIS DAUBIGNY,
Harvest, 1851.
Oil on canvas, 135 x 196 cm.

Below:
ROSA BONHEUR,
Ploughing in the Nivernais Region: first dressing, 1849.
Oil on canvas, 134 x 260 cm.

Marie-Rosalie, known as Rosa, was the daughter of Raymond Bonheur, a painter by profession. Ploughing and harvesting, horses, bulls and cows soon no longer held any mystery for the artist who painted endless vast rural scenes with domestic animals, her famous characteristic subject. Belonging to the same generation, Daubigny gradually focussed so much more on cloudy skies and reflections in water that he had a boat converted into a floating studio to sail over his central theme.

STUDIO IMAGES

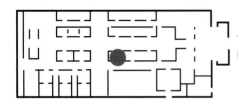

These works are situated on the ground floor, in room 6.

CAMILLE COROT,
Corot's Studio, circa 1865.
Oil on canvas, 56 x 46 cm.

CAMILLE COROT,
Dance of the Nymphs, circa 1860-1865.
Oil on canvas, 47 × 77.5 cm.

The artist uses his studio as a stylistic device. It is his way of showing who he is, how he wants to be perceived, how he works, and the social standing that he has achieved. So many artists, so many images: the cluttered studio, colourful bric-a-brac crammed with plaster casts and skulls, painted to shock bourgeois attitudes; then the more refined studio-sitting room, where the artist receives his dealer or mistresses; and, lastly, the studio-laboratory, a bare space where few are allowed to enter. One can find Corot's studio at 58, rue du Faubourg-Poissonnière.

RURAL ICONS

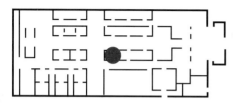

These works are situated on the ground floor, in rooms 5 and 6.

JEAN-FRANÇOIS MILLET,
The Gleaners, 1857.
Oil on canvas,
83.5 × 111 cm.

Sometimes paintings are so overused that they become almost trite and impossible to appreciate. Who can now stand in front of *The Gleaners or The Angelus*, rural landscapes painted by Millet, without all the different objects on which they were reproduced suddenly springing to mind? (from post-office calendars to wall-hangings; earthenware plates to camembert boxes). We therefore have to fight our way through these images to reach the painting itself, and follow the monumental rhythm of the three stooping figures, sustained by the yellow ochre, the orange-tinged pinks and the sky blue of the head-dresses.

JEAN-FRANÇOIS MILLET,
Spring, 1868-1873.
Oil on canvas,
86 × 111 cm.

JEAN-FRANÇOIS MILLET,
The Angelus, 1857-1859.
Oil on canvas,
55.5 × 66 cm.

PORTRAIT OF A VILLAGE

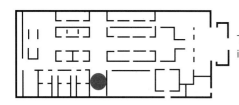

This work is situated on the ground floor, in room 7.

GUSTAVE COURBET,
The Burial at Ornans, 1849-1850.
Oil on canvas, 315 x 668 cm.
The original title was
Scene of human figures,
depicting a burial at Ornans.

Here the painter sets himself the task of painting the portrait of the inhabitants of his village, turning an image of peasants into a history painting. His letters describe his labour. October 30, 1849, sorting out problems at his studio: "My father had a fairly respectably sized studio built for me, but the window was too small [...]. I immediately had one three times as big put in; there is now as much light as out in the street." November 26, trying not to lose heart: "I still have 20 feet 2 inches left to paint, or 30 to 40 figures." February-March 1850, taking stock: "The following have already sat: the mayor, the priest, the justice of the peace, the cross bearer, the lawyer, deputy Marlet, my friends, my father, the choirboys, the gravedigger, two old veterans of the '93 Revolution dressed in period clothes, a dog, the corpse and pallbearers, the vergers (one of whom has an enormous bright red nose, 5 inches long [...]". July 31, the exhibition: "A good two thousand peasants came to Ornans to see my paintings."

A REALIST PROJECT

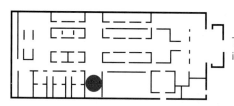

This work is situated on the ground floor, in room 7.

GUSTAVE COURBET, *The Artist's Studio. A Real Allegory Summing up Seven Years of My Life as an Artist,* 1854-1855, exhibited in the "Realism Pavilion", Place de l'Alma. Oil on canvas, 361 × 598 cm.

Detail: the model, the artist and Charles Baudelaire.

FÉLIX TOURNACHON, know as NADAR, *Portrait of Charles Baudelaire Seated on a Louis XIII Armchair,* circa 1855. Salt print from a glass negative, 21.2 × 16.1 cm.

A Jew, a priest, a 1793 republican, a hunter, a reaper, a Herculean figure, a jester, an old-clothes man, a worker and his wife, an undertaker's assistant, a skull, an Irish woman and a model… These are, according to the artist, the figures depicted on the left-hand side of his painting. Continuing his description, he points out to the right a few friends, a collector, a philosopher, a critic, and lovers, not forgetting a poet, Baudelaire. "It is the physical and moral history of my studio," Courbet stated in 1854, "these are the people who live on life, who live on death. This is society at its highest, lowest, and middle echelons. In a word, this is my way of perceiving society in its interests and passions. It is the world that came to be painted in my studio."

BEYOND INTIMACY

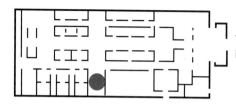

This work is situated on the ground floor, in room 7.

GUSTAVE COURBET,
Origin of the World,
1866. Oil on canvas,
46 × 55 cm.

While Courbet's nudes often created a scandal, revealing their solid anatomies shamelessly and without the slightest mythological pretensions, this was not at all the case for the obscure *Origin of the World*. This is because it was created not to be exhibited, but to become an object of private devotion, a secular, sexual icon exclusively reserved for a collector, the Turkish diplomat Khalil-Bey. It was for him that the image was re-centred and squeezed into a close-up of something that was never seen in a painting.

GUSTAVE COURBET,
Man Wearing a Leather Belt.
Self-Portrait, 1846.
Oil on canvas, 100 × 82 cm.

Right page:
GUSTAVE COURBET,
The Spring, 1868.
Oil on canvas, 128 × 97 cm.

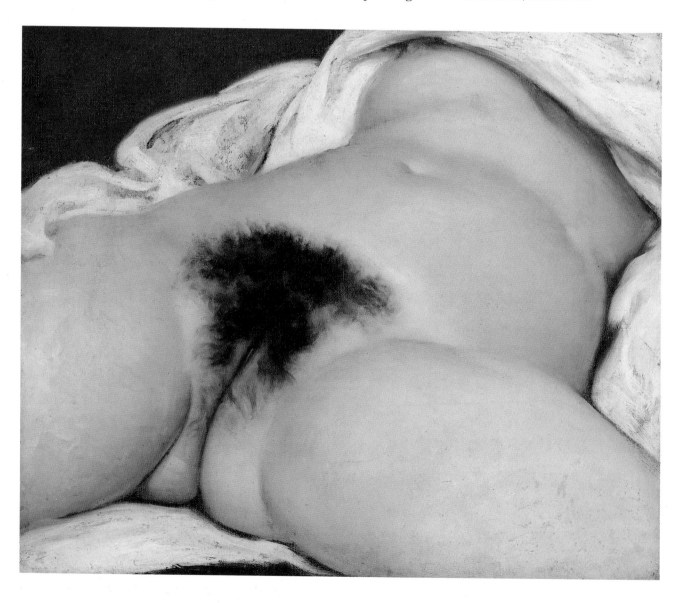

OFFICIAL ART

IMPERIAL VENUS

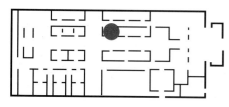

These works are situated on the ground floor, in room 3.

1863 was a year of contrasts. The creamy pink allure of the languishing Venus was widely acclaimed at the *Salon* (official exhibitions of the French Royal Academy of Painting and Sculpture founded in the 17th century), and made such an impression on Napoleon III that he immediately purchased the painting. An essay was published that same year, destined to have decisive influence. Thus appeared *The Painter of Modern Life* by Charles Baudelaire, which lauds the beauty of the modern world, its customs and morals, and which then utterly opposes the mythological, historical, anecdotal genre of Alexandre Cabanel, official artist, professor at the *École des Beaux-Arts*, and member of the Academy.

ALEXANDRE CABANEL,
Death of Francesca de Rimini and Paolo Malatesta,
1870. Oil on canvas, 184 × 255 cm.

Right page:
ALEXANDRE CABANEL,
The Birth of Venus, 1863.
Oil on canvas, 130 × 225 cm.

IN VOGUE

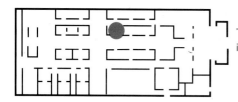

These works are situated on the ground floor, in room 3.

CHARLES DURANT, known as CAROLUS-DURAN,
Lady with Glove, 1869.
Oil on canvas, 228 × 164 cm.

Right page:
FRANZ XAVER WINTERHALTER,
Mme Barbe de Rimsky-Korsakov,
1864. Oil on canvas, 117 × 90 cm.

JAMES TISSOT,
Portrait of Mlle L.L. or *Young Woman in a Red Jacket,*
1864. Oil on canvas, 124 × 99.5 cm.

Crinolines, white muslin, flounced skirts, silks set off with pompons, boned low-cut bodices, sleeves trimmed with the finest fabrics, harmonies of blues and greens, white gloves and a flower pinned in the hair: such was the elegance of evening dress during the Second Empire. This was the type of fashion adored by Théophile Gautier in 1858: because if artists "mixed more often in elegant society and cast aside their studio prejudices for one evening, they would see that evening dress is capable of pleasing even the most fastidious, and that the painter who would care to treat this subject in a historical capacity, applying his style, without being any the less scrupulous, would arrive at astonishing effects of beauty, elegance and colour."

SHOWING AT THE SALON

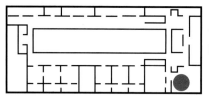

These works are situated on the middle level,
in rooms 51 and 53.

HENRI GERVEX,
*Session of the Painting Jury
at the Salon des Artistes Français,
in a room on the first floor of
the Industrial Design Pavilion,*
1885. Oil on canvas,
299 × 419 cm.

WILLIAM BOUGUEREAU,
The Birth of Venus, 1879.
Oil on canvas, 300 × 215 cm.

Because it had been holding art exhibitions since the beginning of
the 18th century, the *Salon Carré du Louvre* gave its name to an in-
stitution which would be the subject of great discussion a century later.
The *Salon* became the place where an artist's career was at stake,
where the Paris smart set would congregate, from critics to prospective
clients: to exhibit there meant that an artist existed, that he would
be talked about, even at the price of a scandal, and that he would
sell. The jury refused to allow any deviation from the rules of official art. Several artists were excluded, but the record was undoubt-
edly reached in 1863 when, out of the five thousand works submitted,
three thousand were rejected. Artists gradually came to organise
their own exhibitions, and the 1880s saw the creation of other less
narrow institutions, with the *Salon des Artistes Français* (exhibitions
of the French Artists Society) followed by the *Salon des Indépendants*
(exhibitions of the Independent Artists Society).

DELIGHTFUL DECADENCE

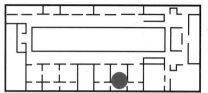

These works are situated on the middle level, in room 57.

GIOVANNI BOLDINI,
Mme Charles Max,
1896. Oil on canvas,
205 × 100 cm.

JACQUES ÉMILE BLANCHE,
Marcel Proust,
1892. Oil on canvas,
73.5 × 60.5 cm.

Right page:
GIOVANNI BOLDINI,
*Count Robert
de Montesquiou*,
1897. Oil on canvas,
160 × 82.5 cm.

After meeting Count Robert de Montesquiou-Fezensac in 1893, Marcel Proust was full of praise for his "professor of beauty", this "delightful decadent", this prince of turn-of-the-century Parisian elegance, aesthete and interpreter of symbolist art. In fact, in his work *Remembrance of Things Past*, the author was greatly inspired by him, namely in his character, the Baron de Charlus. Far from being flattered by seeing himself in the said baron, the Count retorted by painting a rather spiteful portrait of Proust and his novel: "To start with, it is an autobiography of sorts," he wrote in his memoirs, "where there are some nice parts, which he wantonly and almost sadistically intersperses with dreadful parts, since the former are family memories, and the latter, scenes of sapphism, the whole thing ending in utter confusion, for want of structure, taste and choice."

IMPRESSIONISM

A BATHING SCENE CREATES A STORM

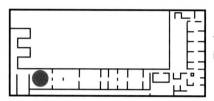

These works are situated on the upper level,
in room 29.

ÉDOUARD MANET,
Blond Woman with Bare Breasts,
circa 1878. Oil on canvas,
62.5 × 52 cm.

ÉDOUARD MANET,
The Picnic,
exhibited in 1863 at the *Salon des Refusés*
under the title *"Bathing"*.
Oil on canvas, 208 × 264 cm.

In 1863, crowds curious to see the work of artists excluded from the official *Salon* swept through the doors of the "Salon des Refusés". A certain work known as *"Bathing"* caused a scandal, both due to its subject matter – the model was naked while the gentlemen were fully clothed – and the artist's technique – considered loose and unrefined; furthermore, it was questionable whether the painting was actually finished. Twenty years later, in his novel *The Masterpiece*, Émile Zola was inspired by the sarcastic remarks which erupted concerning his friend Manet's painting: "Now then, the woman is too hot, but the gentleman is wearing his velvet coat in case he catches a cold. – Oh no, she has already turned blue, the gentleman dragged her out of the pond, and he is resting at a distance, holding his nose. – How rude! He could have at least tried not to sulk."

EMPHASISING AND CENTRING

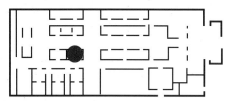

These works are situated on the ground floor, in room 14.

ÉDOUARD MANET,
The Fife Player,
1866. Oil on canvas,
161 × 97 cm.

ÉDOUARD MANET, *The Balcony,* 1869. Oil on canvas, 170 x 124 cm. Models: Berthe Morisot, painter Antoine Guillemet, violinist Fanny Claus and, in the background, Léon Leenhoff.

"Paint realistically, never mind what people say": this was one of the precepts of Manet's art and career. To paint realistically was to belong to one's own time, to choose modern scenes, but also to construct a painting in which nothing happened – four figures, a dog, a flowerpot -, or even to emphasise a figure on a neutral background. To ignore what people said meant not to listen to those disparaging voices, to those who were disconcerted by the absence of anecdotal subject matter.

UNDER THE GAZE OF THE MODEL

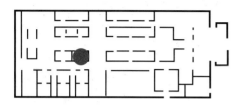

These works are situated on the ground floor, in room 14.

Imagine the laughter, anger, scorn and hatred provoked, in the *Salon* of 1865, by the peculiar image of a woman lying on a bed, not lifeless but slightly upright and looking at her observers. *Olympia* received all the insults imaginable, because this "perfectly ugly", "yellow-bellied odalisque" was none other than a Parisian prostitute of the time. Not one of the revealing, lewd details was overlooked: a ribbon around her neck emphasising her nudity, a slipper, the central position of her hand, even the servant bringing in a bouquet of flowers - perhaps a token from some client - and then the cat, this "black cat leaving its muddy pawprints on the bed" (Théophile Gautier).

ÉDOUARD MANET, *Émile Zola*, 1868.
Oil on canvas, 146 × 114 cm.

ÉDOUARD MANET, *Olympia*, 1863.
Oil on canvas, 130 × 190 cm.

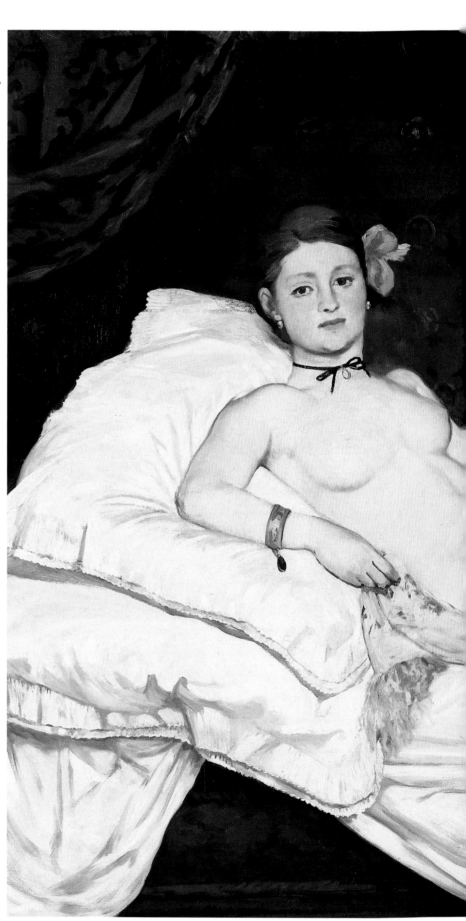

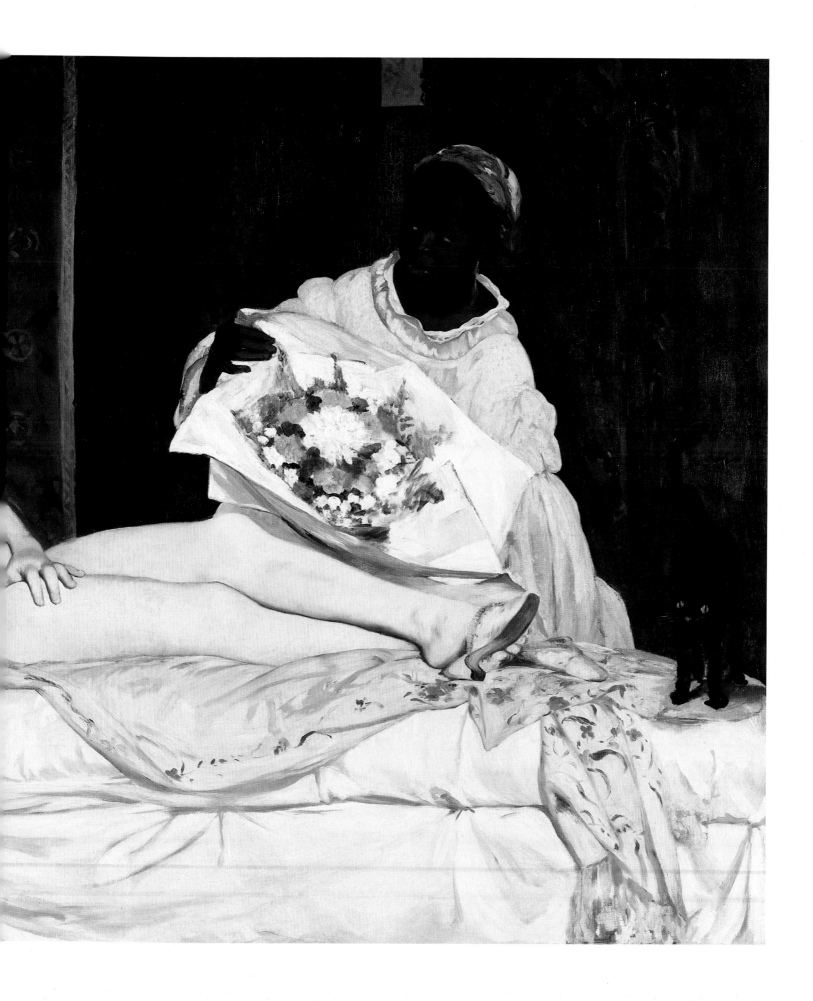

IN THE BATIGNOLLES

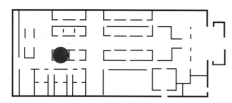

These works are situated on the ground floor, in room 18.

Opposite:
HENRI FANTIN-LATOUR,
The Studio in Les Batignolles, 1870.
Oil on canvas, 204 × 273 cm.

From left to right:
Otto Scholderer, Édouard Manet,
Auguste Renoir, Zacharie Astruc,
Émile Zola, Edmond Maître,
Frédéric Bazille and Claude Monet.

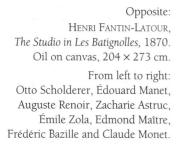

FRÉDÉRIC BAZILLE,
Bazille's Studio, 1870.
Oil on canvas, 98 × 128 cm.

By the staircase:
Auguste Renoir and Émile Zola
(or Claude Monet and Alfred Sisley).
By the easel:
Claude Monet (or Zacharie Astruc),
Édouard Manet and Frédéric Bazille.
At the piano: Edmond Maître.

On the Right Bank of the new Paris, planned and improved by Baron Haussmann, the Batignolles quarter was the meeting place of a younger generation of artists. These advocates of a "new art", these "modernists", were soon to become known as the "impressionists". It was here that they came to pay homage to Manet, to this quarter, loved so much by the master that, in 1870, he moved his studio to 51, rue de Saint-Pétersbourg. Bazille was not far away at 9, rue de La Condamine. Discussions in front of the canvases were often followed by those in the cafés: Friday evening at the Café Guerbois, 11, avenue de Clichy, or at the Café de la Nouvelle-Athènes, 9, place Pigalle.

PAINT IN TUBES

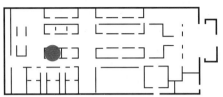

This work is situated on the ground floor, in room 18.

CLAUDE MONET,
The Picnic, 1865-1866,
central fragment of the work,
which had been damaged by damp and
then cut out by the artist in 1884.
Oil on canvas, 248 × 217 cm.

Railways and paint in tubes: two industrial revolutions were to change the lives of these artists who, in the 1860s, wanted to work directly from nature. The steam trains, which took them to the outskirts of Paris, the countryside and the sea, were growing in number. Their easels on their backs, they could now fill their paintboxes with small, pliable, tin tubes of pigments mixed with oil. They now had everything they needed to paint in the open air. At Chailly-en-Bière, in the forest of Fontainebleau, the young Claude Monet watched the light scatter blue-tinged patches over a white expanse.

RECAPTURING THE NOISE AND FURORE

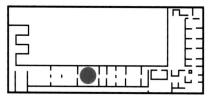

These works are situated on the upper level, in room 32.

In the early days of the Third Republic, a new style of architecture gradually grew up in Paris, showing off its structure and making use of metal frames and glass panels: train stations, department stores, industrial design pavilions and, soon, the Eiffel Tower. The new regime also needed recognition. The creation of a national holiday provided the opportunity for the tricolour to be waved in the streets. Perhaps an observer of his time, certainly an advocate of a new type of representation; here, the painter obscured his subject with clouds of smoke, and there, streaked and marked his canvas with red, recapturing blurred, rapid and ephemeral perception.

CLAUDE MONET,
Rue Montorgueil, National Holiday, June 30, 1878,
1878. Oil on canvas, 81 × 50.5 cm.

CLAUDE MONET,
Saint-Lazare Railway Station, 1877.
Oil on canvas, 75.5 × 104 cm.

THE FIRST IMPRESSION

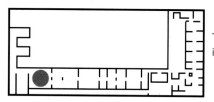

These works are situated on the upper level, in rooms 29 and 34.

Louis Leroy was very fortunate. By ridiculing one of Monet's paintings exhibited in 1874, under the title *Impression, Sunrise*, and baptising an art movement in his own venom, this critic made his name stick. "I also thought to myself," he scornfully remarked in *Charivari*, "perhaps since I was "impressed", there must be some "impression" in it… And what freedom, what looseness in his technique! Even wallpaper in its embryonic state is more developed than that seascape!" The impressionists, who had only recently completed their studies, continued to paint their "impressions" facing the light, facing forms turning hazy in a field dotted with red, or a silhouette standing against the sunlight.

CLAUDE MONET,
Poppies,
1873. Oil on canvas,
50 × 65 cm.

CLAUDE MONET,
*Study of a figure
in the open air.
Woman holding an umbrella
turning towards the left*,
1886. Oil on canvas,
131 × 88 cm.

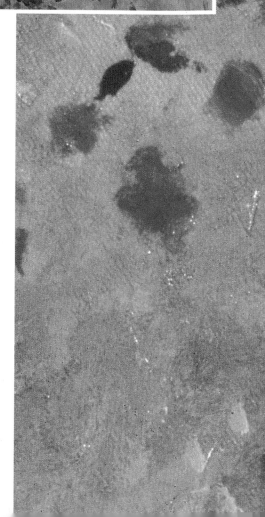

PAINTING IN SERIES

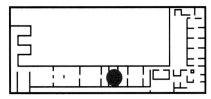

These works are situated on the upper level,
in room 34.

To choose a single motif and repeat it tirelessly, at dawn or at the end of the afternoon, through the changing seasons, in stifling heat or lashing rain: such was Monet's desire, leading him to paint in series. "I am battling on, steadfastly painting a series of different effects," he wrote in a letter dated October 7, 1890, "but the sun goes down so quickly at this time of year that I can hardly capture it… I am working at such a slow pace that I am driven to despair. But the more I advance, the more I can see how difficult it is to convey what I am feeling: "immediacy", especially the same enveloping light shed over everything, and more than ever before, I am repelled by simple things that come all at once."

CLAUDE MONET,
Rouen Cathedral,
Main Door and Saint-Romain Tower,
Full Sun, Harmony of Blue and Gold,
1893. Oil on canvas, 107 × 73 cm.

CLAUDE MONET,
Rouen Cathedral,
Main Door, Morning Sun,
Harmony of Blues, 1893.
Oil on canvas, 91 × 63 cm.

CLAUDE MONET,
Rouen Cathedral,
Main Door, Front View,
Harmony of Browns, 1894.
Oil on canvas, 107 × 73 cm.

WATERSCAPES

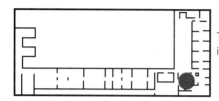

These works are situated on the upper level, in room 39.

CLAUDE MONET,
Blue Water Lilies, circa 1916-1919.
Oil on canvas, 200 × 200 cm.

CLAUDE MONET,
Lily Pond, Harmony of Pinks,
1900. Oil on canvas, 89.5 × 100 cm.

From the 1890s until his death in 1926, Monet's house and garden at Giverny became the subject and focal point of his work. He acquired a piece of land, diverted a river, dug ponds, built bridges, designed flower gardens and grew countless poetic water lilies on the surface of the ponds. Stéphane Mallarmé sent the painter a quatrain in his honour, written on an envelope:

> "Monsieur Monet, whose sight neither winter
> Nor summer deceives
> Lives at, and paints, Giverny
> Near Vernon, in the region of Eure."

The poet admired the waterscapes created by Monet.

CLAUDE MONET,
The Artist's Garden at Giverny, 1900.
Oil on canvas, 81 × 92 cm.

FEMININE IN THE PLURAL

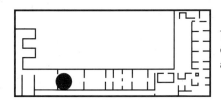

These works are situated
on the ground floor, in room 19,
and on the upper level, in room 30.

ÉDOUARD MANET,
Berthe Morisot with Bouquet of Violets,
1872. Oil on canvas, 55 × 38 cm.

MARY CASSATT,
Woman Sewing in a Garden,
circa 1880-1882.
Oil on canvas, 92 × 63 cm.

Right page:
BERTHE MORISOT,
The Cradle, 1872.
Oil on canvas, 56 × 46 cm.

While it was usual for a young woman from a good family to devote herself to painting in the same way that she would do cross-stitch or play the piano, it was evidently another matter for her to establish herself as an artist and exhibit alongside her peers, impressionists or not. Things were scarcely any easier in other fields. The first female to pass the *Baccalauréat* was congratulated in 1861; the first female arts student was admitted to the Sorbonne in 1883; 1867 marked the beginnings of secondary education for girls, which was eventually instituted in 1880, and the *Ordre des Avocats* admitted its first female member in 1900, followed by the *Ordre des Médecins* in 1904. However, for young women who did not come from a good family, it was an entirely different matter…

PLANING SPACE

These works
are situated
on the upper level,
in room 30.

By deciding to show *The Planers* at the second "impressionist exhibition" in 1876, Caillebotte joined the ranks of the uncompromising, renegade painters. Faced with the painting, criticism was divided between the social aspect and spatial reflections… Philippe Burty, a realist, applauded this "faithful representation of working life". Others were less enthusiastic, taking offence at the use of perspective: the projecting view distorts everything, the lines of the floor rise vertically, and nothing can be seen beyond the base of a wall and the motif of a balcony. What, then, is so interesting about an image such as this?

GUSTAVE CAILLEBOTTE,
Self-Portrait, circa 1889.
Oil on canvas, 40.5 × 32.5 cm.

GUSTAVE CAILLEBOTTE,
The Planers, 1875.
Oil on canvas, 102 × 146 cm.

BLUE-TINGED LIGHT

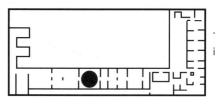

These works are situated on the upper level, in room 32.

PIERRE-AUGUSTE RENOIR,
Dancing at the Moulin de la Galette, 1876.
Oil on canvas, 131 × 175 cm.
Detail on next double page.

FRÉDÉRIC BAZILLE,
Portrait of Renoir,
1867. Oil on canvas,
62 × 51 cm.

PIERRE-AUGUSTE RENOIR,
Study: Nude in the Sunlight,
circa 1876. Oil on canvas,
81 × 65 cm.

There is blue everywhere. The ground is strewn with indigo, a dark blue with violet or reddish tints. Blue-tinged brushstrokes mark the torso of a woman whose pink and, sometimes, red skin catches the light so effectively. Elsewhere, a face has become almost purple, almost unrecognisable, and a dress is covered with long glistening stripes. There is blue everywhere, which, created by the light, colours the shadows: for Renoir, a nude in the sunlight or dancers swirling round one Sunday at a dance at Rue Lepic in Montmartre are mere studies on the dissolution of forms or decomposition of colour.

THE PAINTER'S EYE

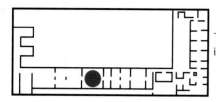

These works are situated on the upper level, in rooms 32 and 34.

Right page:
PIERRE-AUGUSTE RENOIR,
The Swing, 1876.
Oil on canvas, 92 × 73 cm.

PIERRE-AUGUSTE RENOIR,
Young Girls at the Piano, 1892.
Oil on canvas, 116 × 90 cm.

Many critics went to all sorts of lengths trying to make Renoir and his comrades out to be fools. According to Joris-Karl Huysmans in 1880, "Study of the paintings was essentially a physiological and medical concern. I will not mention any names, but suffice to say that, in most cases, their eyes were suffering from the effects of an obsessive fixation. For one, a greyish blue clouded the whole of nature, and a river took on the appearance of a wash tub. For another, there was nothing but purple: land, sky, water, flesh, everything in his work bordered on lilac and aubergine. Most could confirm Dr Charcot's experience of the deteriorating perception of colour observed in many of the lunatics in the Salpêtrière asylum and also regarding the number of people suffering from nervous disorders. Their retinas were diseased…"

IN THE SUN

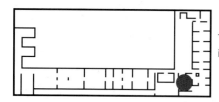

These works are situated on the upper level, in rooms 32 and 39.

Moving to Cagnes-sur-Mer in the South of France in 1903, Renoir continued his explorations, sometimes reaching monumental proportions: he bathes his concentrically rounded female figures in landscapes saturated with colour, abolishes the distance between the curve of a body and an undulating hill, and engulfs a flushed face in vibrating brushstrokes.

PIERRE-AUGUSTE RENOIR,
Women Bathing, circa 1918-1919.
Oil on canvas, 110 × 160 cm.

PIERRE-AUGUSTE RENOIR,
Woman Reading, circa 1874-1876.
Oil on canvas, 46.5 × 38.5 cm.

EFFECTS OF WINTER

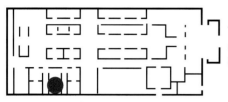

These works are situated
on the ground floor, in room 20,
and on the upper level, in room 32.

Camille Pissarro,
Red Roofs, Corner of the Village, Effects of Winter,
1877. Oil on canvas, 54.5 × 65.6 cm.

Camille Pissarro,
White Frost, The Old Road to Ennery, Pontoise,
1873. Oil on canvas, 65 × 93 cm.

"Furrows?! Frost?!... Those are marks left by a palette scraped across a soiled canvas. There is no beginning or end, top or bottom, front or back." This type of comment, made in 1874 in front of *White Frost*, clearly demonstrates the huge difference between perception at the turn of the 19th century and today. The former was disturbed and shocked by this way of painting stripped down to the essential, and by the wide brushstrokes, juxtaposing and superimposing colour to convey the traces of frost on the ground. Today in the 20th century, the eye is captivated by this familiar type of image, this sensitivity to the effects of winter. The history of impressionism lies between these two perceptions, now no longer shocking, but widely celebrated.

IN THE COUNTRYSIDE

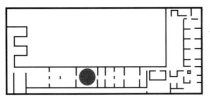

These works are situated on the upper level, in room 32.

CAMILLE PISSARRO,
Approach to the Village of Voisins,
1872. Oil on canvas, 46 × 55.5 cm.

CAMILLE PISSARRO,
Young Girl with Stick,
1881. Oil on canvas, 81 × 64.7 cm.

Voisins, Louveciennes, Pontoise, Éragny-sur-Epte, Auvers-sur-Oise… These villages situated to the north-west of Paris all have one thing in common: they had been the home of Camille Pissarro for many years, after he left Paris through lack of money. They are milestones of sorts in an impressionist journey, which winds through changing landscapes, elements and light, from the forest of Fontainebleau, opening up along the banks of the Marne and the Seine, finally disappearing on the coast of the Channel. As for Pissarro, he lived in and painted the countryside and its inhabitants, in the days when the countryside reached the suburbs.

ATMOSPHERIC BEAUTY

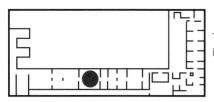

These works are situated on the upper level, in room 32.

ALFRED SISLEY,
Flooding at Port-Marly,
1876. Oil on canvas, 60 × 81 cm.

ALFRED SISLEY,
Road Leading to La Machine, Louveciennes,
1873. Oil on canvas, 54.5 × 73 cm.

Floods, fog, low, heavy clouds, white frost and snow… Alfred Sisley has always been one of the painters most devoted to evoking the beauty of different weather, through the changing seasons over the same landscape. In the words of Henri Matisse, "A Cézanne is a moment with the artist, whereas a Sisley is a moment with nature."

ALFRED SISLEY,
Snow at Louveciennes,
1878. Oil on canvas,
61 × 50.5 cm.

MAD ABOUT HORSES

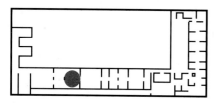

These works are situated on the upper level, in room 31.

EDGAR DEGAS, *The Parade,*
or *Racehorses in front of the Stands,*
circa 1866-1868. Oil on paper
re-mounted on canvas, 46 × 61 cm.

Edgar Degas met Paul Valéry towards 1893. One was almost sixty and the other, barely in his twenties. Forty years later, in 1934, the writer dedicated his work *Degas Danse Dessin* to one who loved art, and also horses: "The Horse walks on points, carried on the tips of its four hooves. No animal can take after the leading dancer, the prima ballerina of the *corps de ballet*, in the same way as a thoroughbred, perfectly balanced, held seemingly suspended by its rider, advancing with quick neat steps in the sunlight. Degas painted an image of the horse in verse:

"All nervously bare in his coat of silk"
in a very well written sonnet in which he indulged himself and did his utmost to focus on the different aspects and functions of a racehorse: training, speed, betting, fraud, beauty and supreme elegance."

EDGAR DEGAS, *The Racetrack,*
Amateur Jockeys near a Carriage, 1876-1887.
Oil on canvas, 66 × 81 cm.

Top:
EDGAR DEGAS, *Rearing Horse.*
Bronze, height: 19 cm.

SCENES OF ORDINARY LIFE

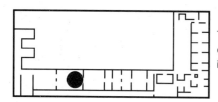

These works are situated on the upper level, in room 31.

EDGAR DEGAS,
In the Café, also known as *Absinthe,*
circa 1875-1876
Oil on canvas,
92 × 68 cm.

EDGAR DEGAS,
Ironers,
circa 1884-1886.
Oil on canvas,
76 × 81.5 cm.

Degas is interested in women. He takes hold of them, outlines them and follows them in their work or rest, finally pursuing them even in their private moments, to the closest point. These women at the turn of the 19th century thus became the heroines of naturalist novels, from *Manette Salomon* by the brothers de Goncourt in 1867 to Gervaise in Émile Zola's *The Dram Shop* ten years later. The same women, posing for Degas, formed an immense repertory of figures: they were washerwomen, ironers or milliners, "madams", prostitutes, singers, actresses, waitresses, dancers and, occasionally, drinkers.

When not truncated, cut off by the frame, decapitated or amputated…, the dancers are sidelined to a corner of the painting to make room for the floors which rise vertically, at the centre of the work. When their bodies are not twisted in exercise, when they are not doubled over at the barre, the dancers are painted from behind in an unattractive pose. Centring and displacing, Degas takes outrageous liberties with his models and representation of space. He only observes or re-creates. This is revealed by his question to an amateur: "Can you arrange for the Opera to give me an entrance ticket for the day of the dance examination, which so I have been told is a Thursday? I feel a bit ashamed because I have done so many of these dance examinations without ever having seen one!"

EDGAR DEGAS,
The Dance Class,
circa 1873-1876.
Oil on canvas,
85 × 75 cm.

Detail on next double page.

DIAGONALS

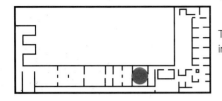

These works are situated on the upper level, in room 36.

PAUL CÉZANNE,
Self-Portrait,
circa 1873-1876.
Oil on canvas,
64 × 53 cm.

In the 1870s, after a period of dark, heavily impasted work, which he later described as "couillarde" and "peinture au pistolet", meaning "bold" and "violent", Paul Cézanne turned to structured landscapes. Everything is constructed, from the brushstroke to the composition, and the painting is split diagonally: "It is like a playing card," he wrote to Pissarro, his friend and master, in 1876. "The sun is so fierce that the objects appear to disappear into silhouettes [...]. Perhaps I mistaken, but this seems diametrically opposed to relief."

PAUL CÉZANNE,
L'Estaque,
circa 1878-1879.
Oil on canvas,
59.5 × 73 cm.

Opposite:
PAUL CÉZANNE,
The Bridge at Maincy,
circa 1879.
Oil on canvas,
58.5 × 72.5 cm.

SLOWLY

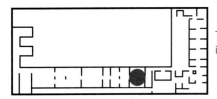

These works are situated on the upper level, in room 36.

PAUL CÉZANNE,
The Card Players, circa 1890-1895.
Oil on canvas, 47.5 × 57 cm.
Detail on previous double page.

Right page:
PAUL CÉZANNE,
Woman with Coffee-Pot, circa 1890-1895.
Oil on canvas, 130.5 x 96.5 cm.

PAUL CÉZANNE,
Bathers, circa 1890-1892.
Oil on canvas, 60 × 82 cm.

Cézanne painted slowly, and the model, whether a sturdily built woman motionless next to a coffee-pot or peasants sitting on either side of a bottle and table, would be asked day after day to have the patience of a… still life. For Cézanne worked on figures in the same way that he approached objects, defining, breaking down and evening out space. Where one expected to see a portrait, rustic imagery or an open-air bathing scene, he conjures up vibrant facets in coloured planes.

GEOMETRY IN COLOUR

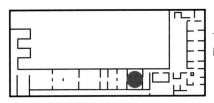

These works are situated on the upper level, in room 36.

PAUL CÉZANNE,
The Blue Vase, circa 1885-1887.
Oil on canvas, 61 × 50 cm.

PAUL CÉZANNE,
Apples and Oranges, circa 1895-1900.
Oil on canvas, 74 × 93 cm.

"In order to move forward, one can only look to nature, which the eye is being trained to perceive. Through constantly looking and working, the eye becomes concentric. What I mean is that in an orange, an apple, a ball or a head, there is a culminating point, and this is always closest to the eye of the painter; edges of objects converge on a central point of the horizon. One does not have to intellectualise one's work to be a great painter. One can do things well without being a great harmonist or colourist. It is enough to have a sense of art. And this is what the bourgeois evidently loathe. Thus, institutes, pensions and honours can only be destined for idiots, fools and clowns. Do not criticise art, paint."

Paul Cézanne, letter to Émile Bernard, July 25, 1904.

POST-IMPRESSIONISM

BALANCE OF OPPOSITES

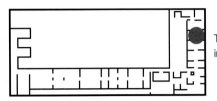

These works are situated on the upper level, in room 45.

GEORGES SEURAT, *The Circus,* 1891.
Oil on canvas, 185.5 × 152.5 cm.

GEORGES SEURAT, *Model From Behind,* 1887.
Oil on wood, 24.5 × 15.5 cm.

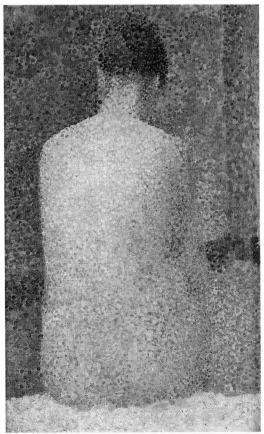

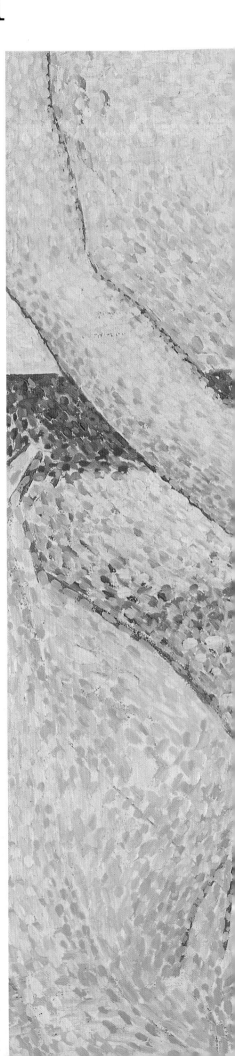

Georges Seurat is a colour theorist and poet: "Art is about balance," he wrote on August 28, 1890. "Balance is the analogy between opposites, likes, tone, hue and line, with the dominant colour and under the effect of light in bright, pale or sombre combinations. The opposites, for tone, are more luminous/light against more sombre tones. For hue, they are the complementary colours, that is, a certain red contrasted with its complementary colour, etc. (red-green; orange-blue; yellow-purple). Lines are contrasted with those making a right angle. The brightness of tone lies in the luminous dominant colour; for hue, the warm dominant colour, and for line, those above the horizontal."

A DIVIDING BRUSHMARK

These works are situated on the upper level, in room 46.

THÉO VAN RYSSELBERGHE,
Man at the Tiller,
1892. Oil on canvas,
60.2 × 80.3 cm.

Right page:
PAUL SIGNAC,
Red Buoy,
1895. Oil on canvas,
81 × 65 cm.

HENRI-EDMOND DELACROIX,
know as HENRI-EDMOND CROSS,
Hair, circa 1892.
Oil on canvas, 61 × 46 cm.

While the "neo-impressionists" preferred the optical combination of colours to mixing pigments on a palette, while they separated and divided their brushmarks to achieve a maximum of luminosity, these "divisionists" also divided the art world. On one side was Signac, author of the book-cum-manifesto *From Eugène Delacroix to Neo-Impressionism*, published in 1899 and dedicated to Seurat. Cross, Pissarro and critic Félix Fénéon were among his followers. On the other side were the cynical or fierce opponents: Paul Gaugin and Émile Bernard ridiculed these "pointillists" who claimed to apply scientific principles to their art, and slaved away painting tiny dots. They struck up a rhyme in their honour dubbed "Ripipointillades"...

THREE COLOURS: YELLOW...

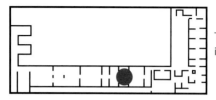

These works are situated on the upper level, in room 35.

VINCENT VAN GOGH, *Eugène Boch*,
Arles, 1888. Oil on canvas, 60 × 45 cm.

VINCENT VAN GOGH, *The Woman of Arles*,
Arles, 1888. Oil on canvas, 92.5 × 73.5 cm.

Right page:
VINCENT VAN GOGH, *The Italian Woman*,
Paris, 1887. Oil on canvas, 81 × 60 cm.

Lemon yellow, golden yellow and ultramarine: from one painting to the next the figures stand out against uniform backgrounds. There is not even the slightest hint of décor to serve as a background or indicate a perspective. Van Gogh thus chose to represent three people who passed through his life. Agostina Segatori is *The Italian Woman*, the proprietress of Le Tambourin, a restaurant on the Boulevard de Clichy in Paris. Madame Ginoux is *The Woman of Arles*, who kept the Café de la Gare, Place Lamartine at Arles. The man in the suit is an artist friend.

THE STUDIO IN THE SOUTH

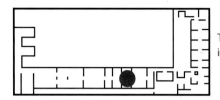

These works are situated on the upper level, in room 35.

When Vincent Van Gogh, a native of Northern Brabant, discovered the city of Arles, this was the start of a dream: to bring other artists here, to establish a studio in the South. He thus writes to his brother Theo in the spring of 1888: "I would like to set up a base for many reasons, a place of rest, to escape from vicious criticism, for worn-out Paris cab-horses, namely yourself and several of our friends, the poor impressionists." He sets about finding a house, large enough to hold a studio. "Then there is my bedroom, which would be extremely plain but with square, wide furniture: bed, chairs and table, all made of pine." Then, he waits. Only Paul Gaugin will join him, and he will stay just two months. His dream of an artists' association will have been a thing of the past.

Vincent Van Gogh,
The Dance Hall at Arles,
1888. Oil on canvas, 65 × 81 cm.

Top:
Vincent Van Gogh,
Self-Portrait,
Saint-Rémy-de-Provence, 1889.
Oil on canvas, 65 × 54.5 cm.

Vincent Van Gogh,
Van Gogh's Bedroom at Arles,
1889. Oil on canvas, 57.5 × 74 cm.
Detail on previous double page.

LETTER TO THEO

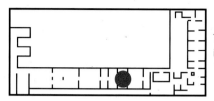

These works are situated on the upper level, in rooms 35 and 50.

VINCENT VAN GOGH,
Hôpital Saint-Paul at Saint-Rémy-de-Provence,
1889. Oil on canvas, 63 × 48 cm.

VINCENT VAN GOGH,
Starry Night, Arles, 1888.
Oil on canvas, 72.5 × 92 cm.

"My dear brother – I always write to you in between working – I am labouring as though truly possessed, I have never before had such a pent-up passion for working. I believe this will aid my recovery. Perhaps I will experience something similar to Eugène Delacroix when he said "I discovered painting when I no longer had teeth nor breath," in the sense that my wretched illness makes me work with a pent-up passion – very slowly – but from morning till evening without respite, and that is probably the secret – to work ceaselessly but slowly."
Vincent Van Gogh,
Letter to Theo,
Saint-Rémy-de-Provence,
September 1889.

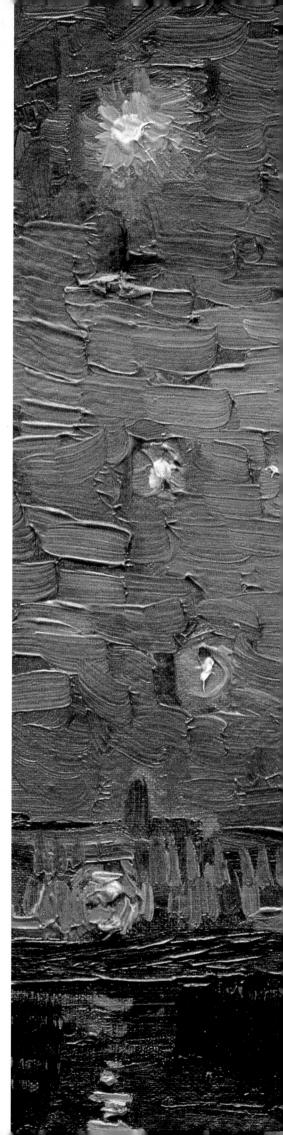

AT AUVERS

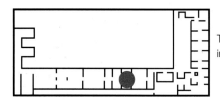

These works are situated on the upper level, in room 35.

Vincent Van Gogh,
Dr Paul Gachet, Auvers-sur-Oise,
1890. Oil on canvas, 68 × 57 cm.

Image of the accursed artist, allegory of the creative genius brushing with madness at every step: Van Gogh quickly became enshrouded in the myth of an eccentric artist, driven to his death in a cornfield in a final battle with his painting. Film-maker Maurice Pialat took hold of this myth and struggled with it, freeing the artist from the debris which had obscured him. The film, made a century after the death of Van Gogh, strives to evoke the final months of the man arriving at Auvers-sur-Oise in May 1890: living a humble existence, in the village, Vincent worked constantly, was often alone, stubborn, determined but full of doubt, hot-headed and finally discouraged.

Vincent Van Gogh,
The Church at Auvers-sur-Oise, View of the Apse,
1890. Oil on canvas, 94 × 74.5 cm.

Vincent Van Gogh,
Two Little Girls, Auvers-sur-Oise, 1890.
Oil on canvas, 51.2 × 51 cm.

VISITS TO BRITTANY

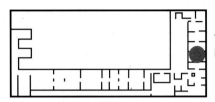

These works are situated on the upper level, in room 43.

PAUL GAUGUIN,
Self-Portrait with Yellow Christ,
1889-1890.
Oil on canvas, 38 × 46 cm.

PAUL GAUGUIN,
The Beautiful Angèle, 1889.
Oil on canvas, 92 × 73 cm.

Impressionism had its own geography winding its way from Argenteuil to Pontoise, following Monet or Pissarro. In the same way, all the different places where Paul Gaugin lived in his search for the exotic, but also through lack of money, can be pinpointed and described. Abandoning Ile-de-France and the banks of the Seine, which had perhaps grown too familiar and already become too busy, in July 1886 he settled at Pont-Aven, in a boarding house run by Marie-Jeanne Gloanec – where many artists already lived - and returned there several times. He then moved further away and, in the winter of 1889-1890, stayed at Le Pouldu, in a hotel kept by Marie Henry, painting portraits of pretty Breton girls. He eventually moved even further away, and arrived in Tahiti on June 9, 1891.

IN MAORI

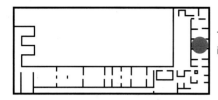

These works are situated on the upper level, in room 44.

PAUL GAUGUIN,
Arearea (Pleasantries),
1892. Oil on canvas, 75 × 94 cm.

PAUL GAUGUIN,
Idol with Pearl, 1893.
Painted, gilt wood
with pearl and gold chain,
h: 23 cm.

While *Noa Noa. Journey to Tahiti*, a manuscript written and illustrated by Gaugin in the 1890s, is a reflection of what he learned and wrote down about a culture, its tales of tutelary gods and spirits, his paintings form a small lexicon of the Maori language and are a poetic representation of ordinary life. *Vahiné no te tiare* is woman with flower, *Te faaturuma* is be silent, mournful and anxious. *Te fare* is the house, *Te matete* the market, *Fatata te miti* is by the sea. *Te nave nave Fenua* describes the delightful earth, *Papa moe*, the mysterious water, and *Te rerioa*, a dream. *Parahi te marae*, there is the temple, *Manao Tupapau*, the spirit of the dead watching. And while *Otahi* is alone, *Noa Noa* is sweet smelling.

LISTENING TO THE SCENT OF HER FLOWER

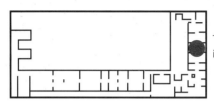

These works are situated on the upper level, in room 44.

PAUL GAUGUIN,
Be Mysterious,
1891. Polychrome wood,
73 × 95 cm.

For a westerner searching for a primitive land, the discovery of the tropics is disappointing: Papeete has been spoilt by this "idiotic colonial civilisation," complains Gaugin, even though approaching one of his first models seems to have been a stroke of luck: "To become properly initiated in the characteristics of a Tahitian face, in the charm of a Maori smile, I had long wanted to paint the portrait of a neighbour who was of genuine Tahitian origin. I asked her one day when she was bold enough to come into my hut and look at photographs of some paintings [...]. I worked quickly, passionately. It was a portrait resembling that which my eyes *veiled by my heart* had perceived. I believe it essentially captured an inner likeness, the subdued strength of a robust fire. She wore a flower by her ear listening to its scent.

PAUL GAUGUIN,
The Meal or The Bananas,
1891. Oil on paper,
re-mounted on canvas,
73 × 92 cm.

Right:
PAUL GAUGUIN,
Tahitian Women
or *On the Beach,* 1891.
Oil on canvas,
69 × 91.5 cm.

IN THE BOIS D'AMOUR

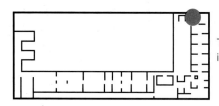

These works are situated on the upper level, in rooms 43 and 48.

ÉMILE BERNARD,
Madeleine in the Bois d'Amour,
1888. Oil on canvas,
138 × 163 cm.

Right page:
PAUL SÉRUSIER,
The Talisman, 1888.
Oil on wood,
27 × 21.5 cm.
Inscription on the back:
"painted in October 1888 by
P. Sérusier, under the guidance of
Gaugin. Pont-Aven."

PAUL SÉRUSIER,
The Shower, 1893.
Oil on canvas,
73.5 × 60 cm.

In the words of Maurice Denis: "It was in the autumn of 1888 that we first heard of Gaugin from Sérusier, when he returned from Pont-Aven and mysteriously showed us the cover of a cigar case upon which one could make out a landscape, formless owing to its "synthetist" construction, in violet, vermilion, Veronese green and other pure pigments, straight from the tube and scarcely mixed with white. "How do you see that tree?" asked Gaugin at a corner of the Bois d'Amour. "Green? Then paint it green, the most beautiful green on your palette. And that shadow? I would say blue. Don't be afraid of painting it as blue as possible." We were thus introduced, for the first time, in a paradoxical and unforgettable way, to the fertile concept of the "flat surface covered with juxtaposed colours". We then knew that every work of art was a transposition, a caricature, the impassioned equivalent of a received sensation…"

THE FOIRE DU TRÔNE

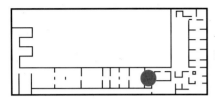

These works are situated on the upper level, in the rooftop gallery and in room 47.

By the turn of the century, artists went out onto the streets; they were accepted in the high places of the Montmartre nightlife, they frequented cafés and music halls, and associated with the young women. Some, namely a certain Henri Marie Raymond de Toulouse-Lautrec-Monfa went so far as to decorate the panels of a booth for La Goulue, the queen of the *"quadrille naturaliste"* or the French cancan (no mean feat), who was to perform an eastern-style dance at the annual Paris fair, the *Foire du Trône*, abandoning her Moulin-Rouge companions, Môme Fromage, Nini-Patte-en-l'Air, Grille d'Égout and Valentin le Désossé. Mesmerised by her extraordinary dancing, the Paris smart set would be there, at her feet.

Henri de Toulouse-Lautrec,
The Female Clown Cha-U-Kao, 1895.
Oil on cardboard, 64 × 49 cm.

Right page:
Henri de Toulouse-Lautrec,
*Dancing at the Moulin-Rouge
(La Goulue and Valentin le Désossé),*
1895. Oil on canvas,
298 × 316 cm.

Henri de Toulouse-Lautrec,
Jane Avril Dancing,
1891. Oil on cardboard,
85.5 × 45 cm.

THE "LADIES" OF THE HOUSE

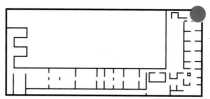

These works are situated on the upper level, in room 47.

HENRI DE TOULOUSE-LAUTREC, *Woman Pulling up her Stocking,* 1894. Oil on cardboard, 58 × 46 cm.

HENRI DE TOULOUSE-LAUTREC, *The Bed,* circa 1892. Oil on cardboard glued to a wooden panel, 54 × 70.5 cm.

Right page: HENRI DE TOULOUSE-LAUTREC, *Woman at her Toilet,* 1896. Oil on cardboard, 67 × 54 cm.

There were numerous houses of ill repute in the 19th century. Lautrec knew them well and, so better to observe his models, he took up residence in one such establishment at 6, rue des Moulins. Although the archaism *"bordel"* ("brothel") was still in use – from the medieval French *"borde"*, or "hut", broad terms or milder euphemisms were often preferred: *maisons publiques, maisons closes, maisons de passe* and *maisons de tolérance.* While there were some more luxurious, comfortable brothels, the *"grandes tolérances"*, there were more seedy establishments which kept *"filles soumises"* or "registered prostitutes" - the *"insoumises"* or "unregistered prostitutes" walked the streets. They generally slept in shared rooms or dormitories, referred to as "kennels" or "henhouses". Two boarders would sometimes share the same bed.

A CUSTOMS OFFICER'S DREAM

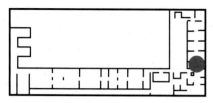

These works
are situated
on the upper level,
in room 42.

"It was after many difficult trials that he managed to make himself known among his contemporaries. He has continued to develop in the original genre that he has made his own, and is in the process of becoming one of our greatest realist painters." This is how the self-taught Rousseau defined and defended his art. He worked as a clerk in the Paris *Octroi* department, and was hence dubbed "Le Douanier" or "customs officer". Artists and poets at the beginning of the 20th century took a strong liking to him: in 1908, Picasso, Max Jacob, Apollinaire, Marie Laurencin, Brancusi and others organised a large banquet in his honour at the Bateau-Lavoir studio, in Montmartre. They paid homage to the great Rousseau, who could conjure up a fantastical warrior or a fantasy tropical exoticism.

HENRI ROUSSEAU, known as
LE DOUANIER ROUSSEAU,
War or *The Ride
of Discord*, 1894.
Oil on canvas,
114 × 195 cm.

Opposite:
HENRI ROUSSEAU, known as
LE DOUANIER ROUSSEAU,
The Snake Charmer,
1907. Oil on canvas,
169 × 189 cm.

A "JAPANESE NABI"

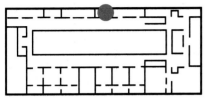

These works are situated
on the upper level, in room 48,
and on the middle level, in rooms 70 and 72.

A colourful *Talisman*, a small piece of nature painted by Paul Sérusier in 1888, won over a group of young painters. They took their name, the "Nabis" from the Hebrew word "*nebiim*" meaning "prophets", and would meet at one of their studios, in the "temple". The words "Talisman", "prophets" and "temple" thus set the tone. According to Maurice Denis, then aged eighteen: "Through

PIERRE BONNARD,
The Checked Blouse,
1892. Oil on canvas,
61 × 33 cm.

PIERRE BONNARD,
Woman Asleep on a Bed
or *Idle Nude,* 1899.
Oil on canvas,
96 × 106 cm.

Below:
PIERRE BONNARD,
Twilight
or *The Game of Croquet,*
1892. Oil on canvas,
130 × 162 cm.

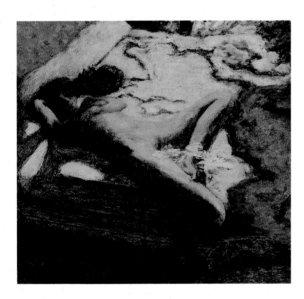

this one word, "nabis", we became the initiated, a sort of mystical secret society; it described the prophetic enthusiasm that was our doctrine." Because he loved off-centre compositions and the flat uniform colours of Japanese prints, Pierre Bonnard became known as the "*nabi japonard*" or "Japanese nabi".

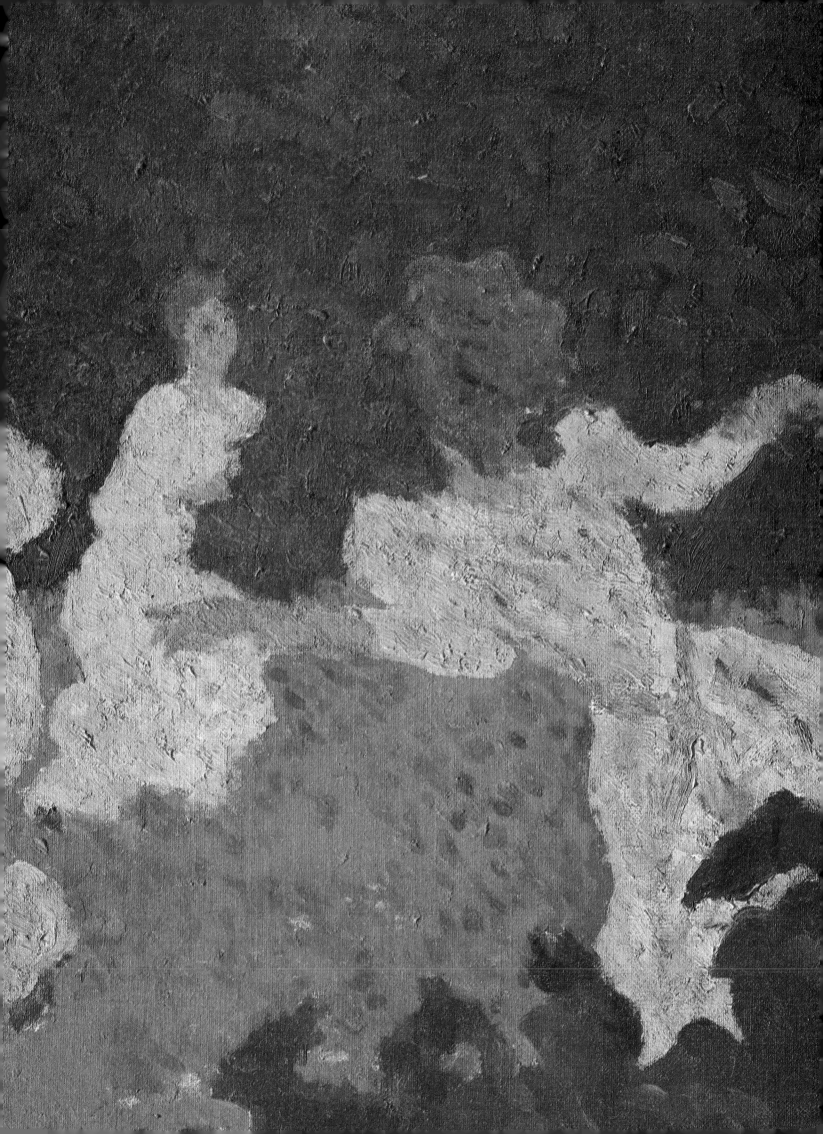

DECORATING LIFE

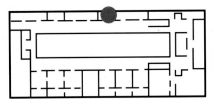

These works are situated
on the upper level, in room 48,
and on the middle level, in room 70.

ÉDOUARD VUILLARD,
In Bed, 1891. Oil on canvas,
73 × 92.5 cm.

Right page:
ÉDOUARD VUILLARD,
The Conversation, 1894,
central panel
of *Public Gardens*,
painted for the dining-room
of Alexandre Natanson's
hotel in Paris.
Glue-based paint on canvas,
213 × 154 cm.

ÉDOUARD VUILLARD,
Profile of Woman with Green Hat,
circa 1891. Oil on cardboard,
21 × 16 cm.

Exploring all the different techniques and textures, from glue-based paint to painting with sand, and attempting to use every type of medium possible, Vuillard was thus dubbed the "Zouave" by his nabi friends. With them he advocated the intrusion of art into life, a lack of distinction between the fine and decorative arts. "Towards the beginning of 1890," reminisced Jan Verkade, "a battle cry was raised, going from one studio to another: no more easel paintings! No more unnecessary furniture! Painting should not usurp the freedom that sets it apart from other arts. The work of a painter starts where that of an architect seemingly ends. Walls should remain surfaces, they should not be broken by images of endless horizons. There are no paintings, only decorations." These decorations took the form of stained glass, wall-hangings, screens and panels adorning a dining-room.

MODERN MUSES

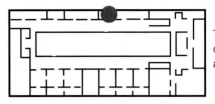

These works are situated
on the upper level, in room 48,
and on the middle level, in room 70.

MAURICE DENIS
(known as "the nabi
of the beautiful icons"),
Sunlight on the Terrace,
1890. Oil on cardboard,
24 × 20.5 cm.

MAURICE DENIS,
The Muses, 1893.
Oil on canvas,
171 × 137 cm.

The Muses were the nine daughters of Zeus and Mnemosyne, the goddess of memory. They lived on Mount Olympus, occasionally attending ceremonies and festivities organised by the gods. However, they spent most of their time offering divine inspiration to musicians and tragedians. These are the divinities of art and science, these are the Muses. Maurice Denis stripped them of their attributes, laurel wreath, flute, viol and compasses... transforming them into turn-of-the-century women.

RED BALL

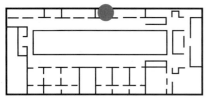

These works
are situated
on the middle level,
in room 70.

The "foreign nabi" paints day and night. At night, he paints a strange self-portrait, facing us and from behind, a massive silhouette dining in the light of a lamp with a black cat running across it. By day, imparting a rightward movement to his composition and long green brushstrokes, he traces the likely path of a small red dot, and suggests a minuscule little girl running in a vast space. So were day and night seen through the eyes of Swiss painter Félix Vallotton.

FÉLIX VALLOTTON,
Dinner, Effects of Lamplight,
1899. Oil on wood,
57 × 89.5 cm.

FÉLIX VALLOTTON,
The Ball, 1899.
Oil on cardboard
mounted on wood,
48 × 61 cm.

INNER REALITY

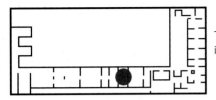

These works are situated on the upper level,
in room 35.

ODILON REDON,
Paul Gauguin, 1903-1905.
Oil on canvas, 66 × 54.5 cm.

Right page:
ODILON REDON,
Closed Eyes, 1890.
Oil on cardboard, 44 × 36 cm.

Odilon Redon chose to be contemporary with his time, the turn of the 19th century. He shared with other symbolist painters the complete rejection of realism, the desire to represent not that which is external, but rather that which suddenly appears when the eyes are closed, by attempting to use, in his words "the logic of the visible to convey the invisible." This may even take the shape of a posthumous portrait, an image of a man who disappeared in the Marquesas Islands in 1903.

NORTHERN VISIONS

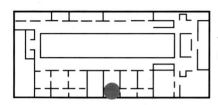

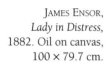 These works are situated on the middle level, in room 60.

JAMES ENSOR,
Lady in Distress,
1882. Oil on canvas,
100 × 79.7 cm.

Right page:
GUSTAV KLIMT,
Roses under the Trees, circa 1905.
Oil on canvas, 110 × 110 cm.

EDVARD MUNCH,
Summer Night at Aasgaardstrand,
1904. Oil on canvas, 99 × 103 cm.

In Belgium, both poets and painters seem to evoke in unison the oppression of unease. Haunted by a fear of madness, Émile Verhaeren transcribes his pessimism in his anthologies, Evenings (*Les Soirs*), Debacles (*Les Débâcles*) and Black Torches (*Les Flambeaux Noirs*); in Hothouses (*Serres Chaudes*), poor torpid soul, Maurice Maeterlinck waits for a little awakening, an end to sleep, a little sun… James Ensor draws yellow curtains over a motionless figure.

The beginning of the 20th century is no longer engrossed in the scandals provoked by the atmospheric beauty captured by the impressionists. Landscapes become the scene of other struggles, whether violent and contrasting in nature, or decorative, as colour gradually consumes the whole painting.

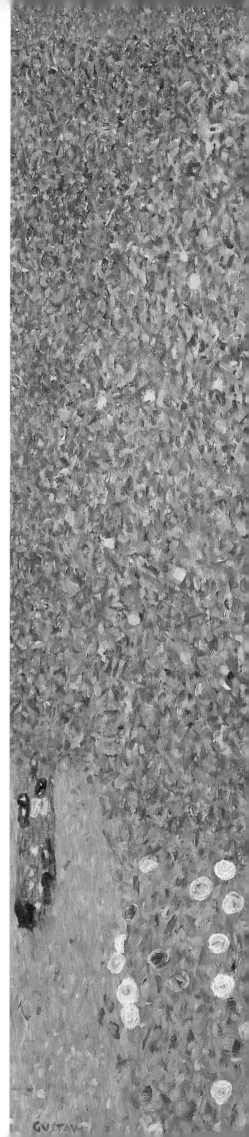

"THERE, THERE IS ONLY BEAUTY AND MEASURE"

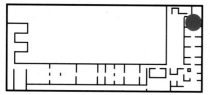

These works are situated on the upper level, in rooms 46 and 50.

ANDRÉ DERAIN,
Charing Cross Bridge,
circa 1906. Oil on canvas,
81 × 100 cm.

HENRI MATISSE,
Luxury, Quietness, and Pleasure,
1904. Oil on canvas,
98.5 × 118 cm.

Henri Matisse read Baudelaire. He knew *Invitation to the Voyage*, from which in 1904 he took a verse to permeate his large canvas with a feeling of fullness. He also must have known the "short poem in prose" which shares the same title. This is "a true earthly paradise, where everything is beautiful, rich, quiet and authentic; where luxury delights to reflect itself in order; where life is sumptuous and sweet to breathe; from which disorder, turmoil and the unforeseen are banished; where happiness is wedded to silence." In 1905, the so-called daubs of Matisse, Derain and other painters would themselves bring about disorder and turmoil.

GRAPHIC ARTS

PENCILS
AND CRAYONS

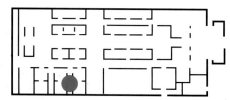

These works are situated
on the ground floor, in room 17.

HONORÉ DAUMIER,
Print Enthusiasts.
Watercolour
tinted with gouache,
lead pencil
and Indian ink,
26 × 31 cm.

Right page:
JEAN-FRANÇOIS MILLET,
The Bouquet of Daisies,
1871-1874.
Pastel, 68 × 83 cm.

It notes the contour of a figure which will find itself in a general composition, it captures a moment, it is a work with its own purpose: an overall view or a specific detail, drawing lends itself to everything. It determines line, sketches in colour, experiments with fluid, oily and dry materials, from ink washes to lead pencils, pastels to graphite, this artificial graphite pencil invented at the end of the 18th century by the engineer Nicolas Jacques Conté.

GUSTAVE COURBET,
Portrait of Juliette Courbet,
Sleeping Child, circa 1841.
Graphite, 20 × 26 cm.

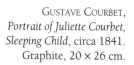

A "PAINTED" PROFILE

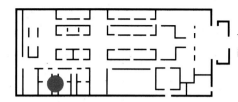

These works are situated on the ground floor, in room 21.

ÉDOUARD MANET,
Irma Brunner,
circa 1880-1882.
Pastel, 53 × 44 cm.

The face has been painted, endowed with a thick pearly sheen, brushed with a creamy softness. This is the face of a pastel portrait. Like his female model, the artist colours his image, softens the contours, powders the cheek, applies lip colour, draws in the eyebrow, uses black to create a buoyant hairstyle, allowing a kiss-curl to form on the forehead, and finally clothes the body in a soft pink. Sophisticated, composed figures, Manet's female subjects were often actresses, painters, such as Berthe Morisot, or *demi-mondaines*, such as Irma Brunner known as *La Viennoise*.

EDGAR DEGAS,
Portrait of Édouard Manet,
circa 1860. Graphite
and Indian ink wash,
35 × 20 cm.

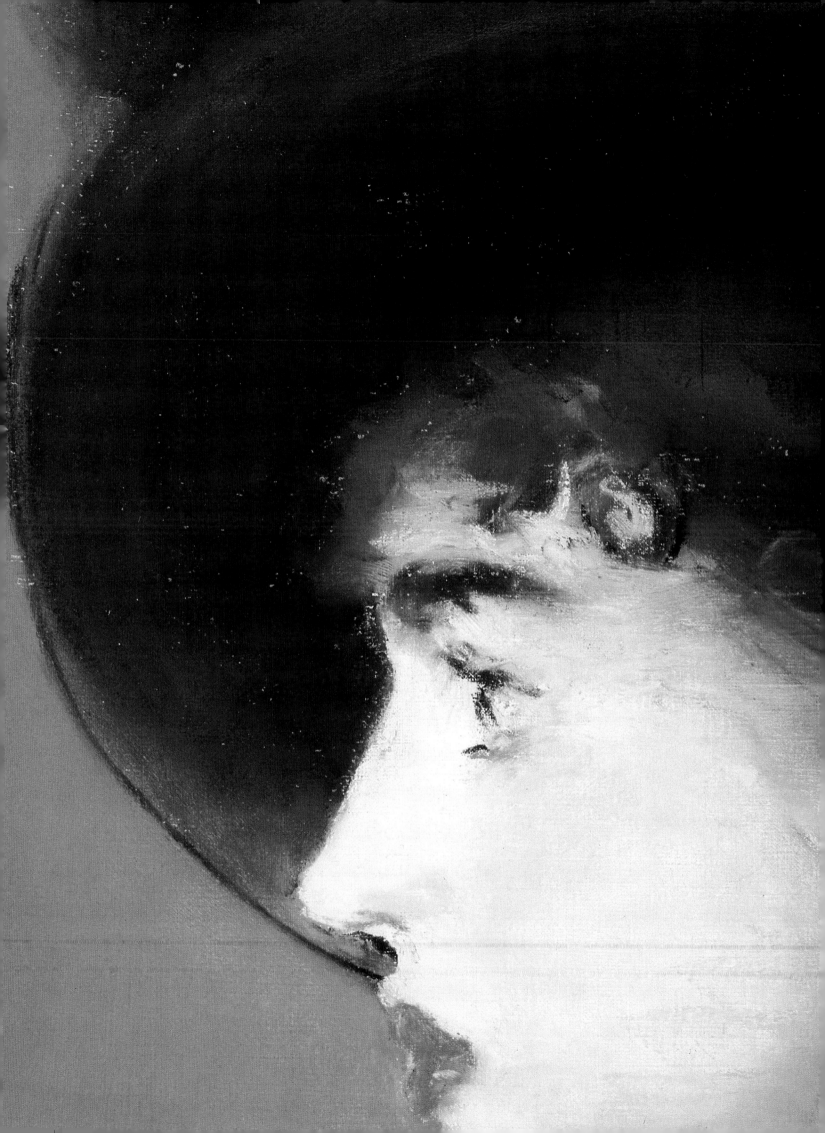

REFLECTIONS AND OPACITY

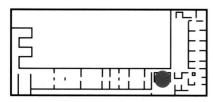

These works are situated on the upper level, in room 37.

Using tempera or oils thinned with spirits, gouache or watercolours and, above all, pastels on paper or grainy cardboard, Degas endlessly experimented with colour and reflections, materials and opacity. Pastels have several virtues: the artist could work quickly or, on the contrary, recapture a gesture, linger over a line. Using hatching and long streaks, superimposing thin layers, and juxtaposing clashing colours, the artist multiplied and reinvented his approach to the female body, captured from different angles, below or above.

EDGAR DEGAS, *The Tub, 1886. Pastel*, 60 × 83 cm.
Part of the *Series of nudes: Women bathing, washing, drying, rubbing down, combing their hair and having it combed*, shown in 1886 at the Eighth Impressionist Exhibition.

EDGAR DEGAS, *Dancer Holding a Bouquet, Taking a Bow on Stage*, 1878. Pastel, 72 × 77.5 cm.

MAKING THE INVISIBLE VISIBLE

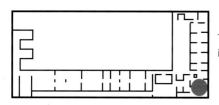

These works are situated on the upper level,
in room 40.

ODILON REDON,
Buddha,
circa 1906-1907.
Pastel, 90 × 73 cm.

Right page:
LUCIEN LÉVY-DHURMER,
Medusa or *Raging Wave*,
1897. Pastel and charcoal,
59 × 40 cm.

ODILON REDON,
The Shell, 1912.
Pastel, 51 × 57.8 cm.

They prefer vision to sight. Their art is tinged with spirituality and plunges into beliefs, myths and legends. For them, woman is often a deadly creature, a poisonous, raging being, a monster of accursed beauty. The world of appearances fades away before the dreamlike universe; the elements come to life, take human form, and become nightmarish figures. They called themselves Symbolists, these painters, draughtsmen and artists who shared the same goal: to make the invisible visible, to cling to fate, dreams, the subconscious and another place. "Anywhere out of the world", such was the motto of Edgar Allan Poe, revived at the close of the century.

PHOTOGRAPHY

SITTINGS

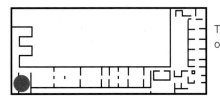

These works are exhibited in rotation on the upper level, in room 49 (level 4).

FÉLIX TOURNACHON, known as NADAR, *George Sand* (detail), 1864. Albumen print.

FÉLIX TOURNACHON, known as NADAR, *Gustave Doré with Drapery*, 1856-1858. Albumen print.

Numerous key figures of the Paris smart set came to sit in Nadar's studio. At eighty years of age, he gathered together a few memoirs from his long experience. In 1900, in his work *When I was a Photographer*, he recollects: "People have such a high opinion of their physical merits that the first impression of all models when presented with prints of their portraits is almost inevitably disappointment and recoil (it goes without saying that in this instance we are only talking about perfect prints). Some of them have the hypocritical sense of propriety to hide their shock by outward indifference, but do not be taken in. They would come in through the door distrustful and aggressive and many would leave utterly enraged. This problem is hard to avoid, and will have to be endured by both amateur and professional photographers alike."

CINEMATOGRAPHY

DECEMBER 28, 1895

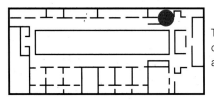

These works are exhibited in rotation on the middle level, in a room located at the far end of the Lille terrace.

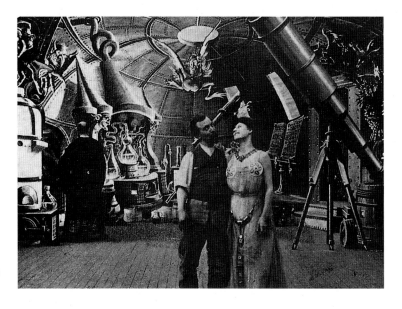

GEORGES MÉLIÈS
in one of his films.

Right page:
AUGUSTE and LOUIS LUMIÈRE,
Place des Cordeliers in Lyon, Tramways,
1895. Frames.

On the evening of December 28, 1895, a programme of ten short films on themes of everyday life was shown at the *Salon Indien* of the Grand Café, 14, boulevard des Capucines: Workers Leaving the Lumière Factory in Lyon, Acrobatics, Fishing for Goldfish, The Arrival of the Photographic Conference in Lyon, The Blacksmiths, The Gardener, Feeding the Baby, The Blanket Toss, Place des Cordeliers in Lyon, and The Sea. A cinematographic show was projected in the *Salon Indien*. Admission: one Franc. "This camera," it was pointed out, "invented by Messrs. Auguste and Louis Lumière, is able to record, in a series of instantaneous frames, all action taking place in front of the lens over a given period of time, and is then able to reproduce this action by projecting life-size images onto a screen, before the entire room." Among the thirty or so spectators, a certain Georges Méliès, then director of the Théâtre Robert-Houdin, would not be one of the least enthusiastic.

DECORATIVE ARTS

PASTICCIO AND MÉLANGES

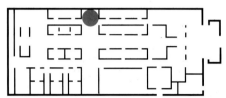

These works are situated on the ground floor, in rooms 9 and 10.

CHRISTOFLE & Cie,
Tray, circa 1870.
Partly gilded, silver-plated
electrolytic copper, d: 29.6 cm.

This tray is part of a gold and silverwork collection, an exact reproduction of the Hildesheim treasure.

Cabinet-makers, jewellers, crockery-makers, enamellers and sculptors, those who worked on the décor and furnishings of homes during the Second Empire, viewed the past as a reliable source of inspiration. This concern for an above all national memory was joined by a taste for tempered exoticism, which was often reflected in the use of precious woods and materials. While one turned to the Middle Ages and imitated Roman gold and silverwork, another discovered and interpreted the lessons of Renaissance ceramists, namely a certain Bernard Palissy. The time is one of allusion, reference and pasticcio.

Top:

FRANÇOIS-DÉSIRÉ FROMENT-MEURICE,
Ewer with tray, item belonging to
the Duchess of Parma's washstand, 1847.
Partly gilded silver,
enamel painted on copper, h: 41.3 cm.

Above:

CHARLES-JEAN AVISSEAU (ceramist)
and GUILLAUME DE ROCHEBRUNE (draughtsman),
Goblet and basin, 1855. Porcelain with
moulded, inlaid polychrome décor,
h (goblet): 34.5 cm; d (basin): 51.5 cm..

Opposite:

CHARLES-GUILLAUME DIEHL (cabinet-maker),
ÉMILE GUILLEMIN (sculptor)
and JEAN BRANDELY (industrial draughtsman),
Cabinet, 1867.
Speckled Maï-du, Honduran mahogany,
Santo Domingo citron wood,
inlaid with sycamore, boxwood
and Saint-Martin Rouge,
constructed in oak, gilded
bronze and electrolytic copper, h: 152 cm.

AN "ARCHITECTURAL ARTIST"

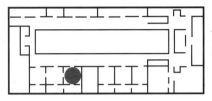

These works are situated on the middle level, in rooms 61 and 62.

HECTOR GUIMARD,
Vase and base, 1905-1907.
Bronze, h: 135.5 cm.

In order to give his work a wider yet more specific definition, Hector Guimard gave himself the unique title of "architectural artist". He would work both on the exterior and interior of a building, from a door to a seat, following the module of vegetal structures with their curves and counter-curves. Today he remains one of the most well known exponents of this international movement which made its début in the mid-1890s: art nouveau. However, the architect preferred a different expression, "*Le Style Guimard*", which caught on at the beginning of the following century referring to his creations at Angers, Lille, Versailles, the entrances to the Paris Métro…

HECTOR GUIMARD,
Folding door from
a gunsmith's shop at Angers,
1897. Walnut, elm, wrought iron
and copper, h: 364 cm.

HECTOR GUIMARD,
Settle, 1897.
Jarrah and basswood, 89 × 151 cm.

A NEW ART FORM

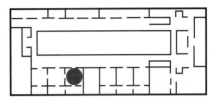

These works are situated on the middle level, in rooms 61 and 62.

Top:
René Lalique, Decorative poppy ornament, 1897. Gold, silver, brilliant diamonds, *plique-à-jour* and *cloisonné* enamel, h: 7.5 cm.

Above:
René Lalique, Dragonfly pendant, 1903-1905. Gold, *plique-à-jour* and *cloisonné* translucent enamel, brilliants and aquamarine, h: 6.9 cm.

Opposite:
Louis Majorelle, Armchair, 1898. Walnut, h: 110 cm.

Below:
René Lalique, *Bonbonnière*, 1904. Gold, *plique-à-jour* and *cloisonné* enamel, opal cabochons, d: 5.5 cm.

At the end of the 19th century, French enthusiasts of this new style of art, soon to be known as *art nouveau*, spoke of this "modern art" and "modern style", when praising the magnificent line of an armchair or the refined charm of a piece of jewellery. As for the cynics, they would use more vivid terms, from "mutton-bone style" to "vulgar vagabond style", or a style inspired by "tape worms", "eels" and "noodles", to describe the arabesques and loops used in the different techniques.

GLASS, THE SEA AND ENAMEL

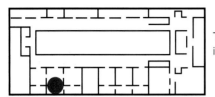

These works are situated on the middle level, in room 63.

ÉMILE GALLÉ,
Flower-holder, circa 1878-1880.
Crackled, "moonlight" glass
with applications,
painted, enamelled and gilt décor,
gilded bronze base, h: 24 cm.

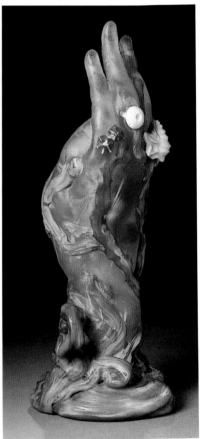

ÉMILE GALLÉ,
Vase, circa 1884. Smoked glass,
enamelled and gilt décor, raised opaque and
translucent polychrome enamel outlined in gold,
h: 32.7 cm. An inscription has been traced
around the neck in enamelled letters:
"À cœur aimant tout possible."

For Marcel Proust, the sea and light flooding into a bedroom are images conjuring up the materials and effects of Émile Gallé's glasswork: "As the season progressed, so changed the picture that I found there in the window. At first, it was broad daylight and only dark in poor weather; then, in the dull blue-green glass, which it swelled with its rounded waves, the sea, fixed between the iron window frames like in the leading of a stained-glass window, would break on the heavy line of rocks in the bay, scattering motionless, plumed foam triangles with the delicacy of a feather or down drawn by Pisanello, and captured by this unctuous, unchanging, white enamel representing fallen snow in Gallés glass," (*Within a Budding Grove, 1918*).

ÉMILE GALLÉ,
"Hand with seaweed and shells",
1904. Engraved crystal, with inclusions
and applications, h: 33.4 cm.

DOWN TO THE SLIGHTEST DETAIL

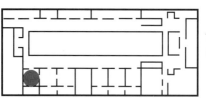

These works are situated on the middle level, in rooms 65 and 66.

HENRY VAN DE VELDE,
Writing desk, model created in 1898-1899.
Oak, gilded bronze, copper and leather, 128 × 268 cm.

ALEXANDRE CHARPENTIER,
Dining-room commissioned for banker
Adrien Bénard's villa at Champrosay, 1990-1901.
Mahogany, oak, poplar and gilded bronze, h: 346 cm.
The glazed stone tiles and flower basin
are the work of ALEXANDRE BIGOT.

In his articles-manifestos of the 1890s, from "Discourse on Art" to "Purification of Art", Belgian painter and architect Van de Velde repeatedly stated that there should be no barriers between the plastic, "noble" arts and the decorative, "applied" arts. This *art nouveau* demanded a new society. As all hierarchy between the different arts had to be banished, so the separation between classes had to be destroyed, a new art form created by and for the people, and the very status of the artist rejected: "It is absurd to speak of inspiration," he wrote, "when it is merely a question of craft." This fusion of the arts and crafts, the quest for "total art" also fascinated Charpentier, who moved from cabinet-making to sculpture, from carving to embossing…

SINGLE PIECES, FACTORY MODELS

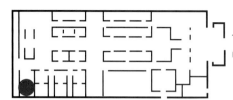

These works are situated in rooms 25 to 27b, reached via room 24, on the ground floor.

In the middle of the century, in London, the Arts and Crafts Movement turned towards the Middle Ages and advocated the industrial distribution of the works of craftsmen; Pugin was one of the major figures of this movement. At the end of the century, in Vienna, the Thonet Frères Firm mass-produced a whole range of inexpensive light, solid and comfortable furniture for cafés and hotels. Chairs, armchairs, sofas and shelves were made from bentwood and laminated wood. Mass-produced, they could be dismantled, and a label bore the following instructions: "In order to maintain the furniture in good condition, please retighten the nuts and screws three or four times a year." Forty-five million No.14 chairs were sold.

AUGUSTE WELBY PUGIN,
Table, circa 1846-1850.
Fir wood and brass, h: 70 cm.

Left:

THONET FRÈRES FIRM,
Chair, model created circa 1905.
Steamed beech, varnished in black,
dyed leather and brass, h: 98.5 cm.

THONET FRÈRES FIRM,
Chair No. 14, model designed in 1849,
purchased by Café Daum, Vienna, in 1850,
and manufactured between 1881 and 1890.
Mahogany-stained, steamed beech, h: 90 cm.

Bottom left:

THONET FRÈRES FIRM,
Chair No. 56, model created in 1885.
Steamed beech, varnished in black,
h: 90 cm.

Below:

CARLO BUGATTI,
Chair, circa 1902.
Parchment-covered wood,
h: 97 cm.

GLASGOW, VIENNA, CHICAGO

These works are situated in rooms 25 to 27b,
reached via room 24, on the ground floor.

CHARLES RENNIE MACKINTOSH,
Dressing-table and looking-glass,
1904. White-lacquered wood,
mother-of-pearl and ebony,
glass and silver-plated brass,
h (total): 179 cm.

Right:
FRANK LLOYD WRIGHT,
Chair, circa 1904.
Stained oak and leather, h: 101 cm.

Below:
JOSEF HOFFMANN,
Reclining armchair,
model created for the
Jacob & Josef Kohn firm,
circa 1908. Steamed beech,
perforated laminated wood,
mahogany-varnish and brass,
h: 110 cm.

Charles Rennie Mackintosh worked in Glasgow. He incorporated furniture that he designed into spaces that he created. In Vienna, Josef Hoffmann was one of the founders of Wiener Werkstätten, an association which produced a wide range of furniture and everyday objects. At the Universal Exhibition in Chicago in 1893, Frank Lloyd Wright discovered Japanese art. In these three cities and through these three architects-decorators-designers, art nouveau took a new course using straight, broken lines in response to the undulating forms predominating in France and Belgium.

RICHLY COLOURED WALLS

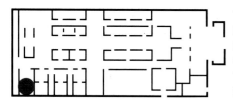

These works are situated
in rooms 25 to 27b,
reached via room 24,
on the ground floor.

The reception room (51)
is situated on the middle level.

WILLIAM MORRIS and WILLIAM DE MORGAN,
Wall-covering panel.
Décor commissioned for Membland Hall,
consisting of eight panels, circa 1876-1877.
Sixty-six glazed earthenware tiles, 163 × 90 cm.

Above and right page:
ODILON REDON,
Wall-covering panel.
Décor commissioned for the dining-room
of the Château de Domecy,
consisting of fifteen panels,
1899-1901. Paint on canvas,
247 × 163 cm.

Whether hanging a wall with wool tapestries, using a motif of earthenware tiles, or arranging panels above woodwork, the process remains the same: pay the same attention to the living environment as to painting a canvas on an easel. However, while Odilon Redon was defined by his status as an artist, William Morris blurred distinctions; painter, and also a poet, he was at the head of a company which produced countless examples of decorative art.

WILLIAM MORRIS & Cº,
Three hangings decorated with birds and floral motifs (detail),
models created in 1878. Wool tapestries.

Next double page:
The reception room of the Hôtel de la Gare d'Orsay, 1898-1900.